Rocking Your Music Business: Run Your Music Business at Home and on the Road

Simon Cann

Course Technology PTR
A part of Cengage Learning
VISUAL & PERFORMING ARTS

COURSE TECHNOLOGY
CENGAGE Learning·

Australia • Brazil • Japan • Korea • Mexico • Singapore • Spain • United Kingdom • United States

COURSE TECHNOLOGY
CENGAGE Learning

Rocking Your Music Business: Run Your Music Business at Home and on the Road
Simon Cann

Publisher and General Manager, Course Technology PTR: Stacy L. Hiquet

Associate Director of Marketing: Sarah Panella

Manager of Editorial Services: Heather Talbot

Marketing Manager: Mark Hughes

Acquisitions Editor: Orren Merton

Project Editor/Copy Editor: Cathleen D. Small

PTR Editorial Services Coordinator: Jen Blaney

Interior Layout Tech: ICC Macmillan Inc.

Cover Designer: Luke Fletcher

Indexer: Larry Sweazy

Proofreader: Kezia Endsley

For product information and technology assistance, contact us at **Cengage Learning Customer & Sales Support, 1-800-354-9706**

For permission to use material from this text or product, submit all requests online at **www.cengage.com/permissions** Further permissions questions can be e-mailed to **permissionrequest@cengage.com**

All trademarks are the property of their respective owners.

Library of Congress Control Number: 2007939366

ISBN-13: 978-1-59863-466-2

ISBN-10: 1-59863-466-6

Course Technology
25 Thomson Place
Boston, MA 02210
USA

Cengage Learning is a leading provider of customized learning solutions with office locations around the globe, including Singapore, the United Kingdom, Australia, Mexico, Brazil, and Japan. Locate your local office at: **international.cengage.com/region**

Cengage Learning products are represented in Canada by Nelson Education, Ltd.

For your lifelong learning solutions, visit **courseptr.com**

Visit our corporate website at **cengage.com**

Printed in the United States of America
1 2 3 4 5 6 7 11 10 09

Acknowledgments

I would like to thank everyone involved with the production of this book, especially Stacy Hiquet and Mark Hughes, and all the good people at Course Technology.

I would particularly like to single out for thanks Orren Merton and Cathleen Small: Orren, for his vision and patience and for many conversations…many of which went nowhere (as well as being the guy who gets me hired), and Cathleen, for steering the book through the production process so smoothly and speedily, in addition to performing editing duties. Thank you both.

About the Author

Simon Cann is a writer based in London. He is the author of a number of music-related and business-related books.

His music-related books include *How to Make a Noise, Cakewalk Synthesizers: From Presets to Power User, Building a Successful 21st Century Music Career, Sample This!* (with Klaus P. Rausch), and *Project5 Power!* His business-related books include the *Made It In...* series of books, which feature the experiences of international entrepreneurs who have built successful companies in the hottest business locations around the world.

You can read more about Simon at his website, simoncann.com, and check out his other music-related books at his Noise Sculpture website, noisesculpture.com. Further information about the *Made It In...* series of books can be found at madeitin.com.

Contents

Chapter 2
Setting Up Your (Virtual) Office   33

Chapter 3
Working with Other People 103

Chapter 4
Running Your Business Online 133

Chapter 5
Accounts, Records, and All Those Pieces of
Paper You Need to Keep   193

Chapter 6
Government and Officialdom: You Ain't Gonna
Fight the Law   205

Introduction

If you want to make a living from your music:

- You need to make money from your music. To use that really ugly buzzword of the moment, you need to "monetize" your music-making activities.

- Even if your primary focus is not on the money, you still need to have a clear understanding of who is doing what, how those things are being achieved, and how the costs are being met. Perhaps most importantly in the highly litigious society in which we all live, you need to know that you are doing things legally and understand who will take the responsibility if something goes wrong.

- Once there is money involved, you need to pay attention. Even if you don't care how much you earn, you still need to ensure that you don't get ripped off.

- Once you start paying attention, you need to focus on the business aspects—not just the money and not just the liabilities, but everything.

You cannot *not* do business—you can only do it badly or not attend to the matters that need your attention. The alternative—if you do not want to pay attention to the business aspects—is to get a proper job so that music is just a hobby. And once you get a proper job, you'll be working in someone else's business, so it won't have gotten you away from that whole business thing anyway.

The tough thing about doing business is that there are several (usually many) elements to doing the business—each element needs to be addressed and completed before you can be successful. Once you start working on your own business, you don't get marks for trying hard—you only get paid when you succeed.

Take a simple example—creating your own CD. Look at some of the interactions you may have:

- You will need to book studio time—at a time that is convenient for you and the studio—and at the end of the process, the studio will need to be paid.

- You will probably hire an engineer, and you may also hire a producer and/or someone to help mix the tracks. You will need to schedule these people at a time that is convenient for you and the studio. These people will also want to be paid, and if you are hiring a producer, then he or she may want a share of the income.

- Once you have your tracks mixed, then you will need to get them mastered. Again, the mastering engineer will want to be paid.

- You can then take your mastered tracks to a CD-pressing plant. Suddenly, you will have a whole bunch of new issues to contend with:

  - Artwork for the booklet (and the CD itself). You will need to pay for this.

  - You may need to credit the engineer, the producer, and the mastering engineer.

  - You will need to include copyright assertions, noting who wrote the tracks, who owns those copyrights, and who owns the sound recording.

- Once you have your finished CD in your hand (and you've paid the pressing plant), you will need to look at distribution. Sure, you can sell the CD at your gigs, but this raises a whole range of other questions, such as how the stock gets there, whether it is insured, how you deal with thefts, and so on.

- Alternatively, you can sell the CD through stores. If you're going to sell through stores, then what terms will you be offering (normal practice is sale or return), and what price will you be charging?

I think you get the idea. Even for something as apparently simple as a CD, there are lots of different elements, and if you fail at any one stage—for instance, at the CD-pressing stage— then the whole project fails.

This book introduces you to business and shows you how to apply business methodology to your music activities. It looks at certain fundamental elements that are common to all businesses:

- The infrastructure—in other words, the tools, such as computers and software, you need to do business.

- The systems and processes you need in place—the things you need to do to make money (and usually you will need to use your infrastructure to help you execute the processes).

- The contracts you may need—the documents that define your relationship with the people with whom you work. As you will see, there are some sample contracts for certain purposes included in the book.

The way that we all do business is changing, and the dividing lines between business and personal, corporate, and consumer are blurring more every day. There are new tools that help us live our lives. These new tools bring huge benefits, especially in terms of linking with other people, but they also bring new challenges.

For most people, the notion of "business" is inextricably linked with an office. You are going need an office; however, this does not need to be the sort of office that your parents or grandparents might have worked in. We're in the 21st century, and we all have many more choices about how we work. Some of those new opportunities fit perfectly with the way that you will probably want to run your music business.

You probably think of an office as being a place that people go every day, and where they are required to wear a suit. For many that is true, but for the musician on the move, the notion of having a business attached to a specific building is an anathema—you want to be out on the road playing to people. As you will read in Chapter 2, there are new tools available—often using the latest cloud computing technologies—and these allow you to set up a business infrastructure that is independent of:

■ Geography. You are not tied to an office or a room. Your office is wherever you are, which is a perfect situation if you are a musician on the road.

■ Software platform. Your office will work the same whether you are a Mac, a PC, or a Linux person.

■ Hardware. While you have to use some hardware, you are not tied to any one specific piece of hardware, so if your laptop dies or you lose your cell phone, business carries on. More than that, you can access your office from a whole range of different pieces of hardware, including:

  ■ Desktop computer

  ■ Laptop computer

  ■ Ultra-portable computer

  ■ Cell phone/Smartphone/PDA

The changes this new technology offers are significant. You can now easily share data with anyone, anywhere. If you are running your music business, this means that you can work with people who are not sitting next to you, so you can get your manager to look at some figures even if he or she is on the other side of the world. Equally, these new options mean that:

■ Your data is more secure. If you lose your computer, it doesn't matter—your data will still be safely stored in the "cloud."

■ Disaster recovery is much quicker. If you lose your computer, you just need to find another computer (for instance, you could go to an internet café), and you will be up and running again.

There is another huge advantage to these new ways of working: The costs are lower, and everything fits with how we live our lives. For instance, if you've got an iPhone or a Smartphone, you can use that to run your office—you don't need to go and buy a new phone. Equally, the cost of using cloud services is often free or very cheap, especially when compared to the cost of conventional desktop office applications.

Your business is important: If you pay attention to it, it will look after you for years to come.

1 Your Music Business

Making money from music is blissfully simple: You make music, you get paid. Well that's the idea, anyway. In practice, people won't put money directly into your bank account. Instead we swap things.... In the old days—the really old days—before television and before electricity, people would exchange what they needed for other things. So a blacksmith might put a shoe on a horse, and the farmer who owned the horse might give the blacksmith some grain by way of payment. This was called bartering.

These days, we have money (although bartering is still good). In order to get money, you have to give people things in return; see Figure 1.1. For instance, they might give you money, and you give them a CD, a T-shirt, or a ticket to your gig tonight.

See, it's easy, isn't it?!?

This is capitalism. To benefit from it—and you need to benefit from it if you're going to put food on your table and keep a roof over your head (or buy that Ferrari you've always wanted)—you need to organize your music-related activities as a business.

This book is about the business aspects of music. It tells you:

- The practical issues you need to attend to—beyond picking up a musical instrument—in order to make money and run your music business.

- How to deal with the practical issues of setting up and running your business. However, this book does assume a certain level of common sense on your part (and I know you have that quality since you are reading this book), hence, it doesn't seek to dot every I and cross every T for every jurisdiction around the world.

Figure 1.1 A fair exchange? Should we go back to bartering?

This first chapter introduces the main themes that will be discussed in the book. In particular, it looks at:

- What is business? Many musicians see their business as "making music"; however, in reality, much of the income generated in the music industry today flows from selling products (such as CDs and T-shirts).

- Infrastructure—in other words, what is necessary to carry out the business? Musicians understand that they need instruments. Beyond that, you need the other tools that are necessary to do the business part.

- People who the musician will come into contact with as part of the business— whether they be other musicians, roadies, professionals such as accountants, studio owners/managers, or gig bookers. How you deal with these people—on a business basis—will have a significant effect on how much you earn.

Music Business History

When people think about the music business, they often think about the "good old days" when it used to be easy: Form a band, play some small gigs, get a record contract, release an album or two, play huge gigs, become an international star, and die in suspicious circumstances (drug-related, the tabloids will speculate) before your 30th birthday.

That was considered an ideal musical career. Thankfully, things are different now (see Figure 1.2).

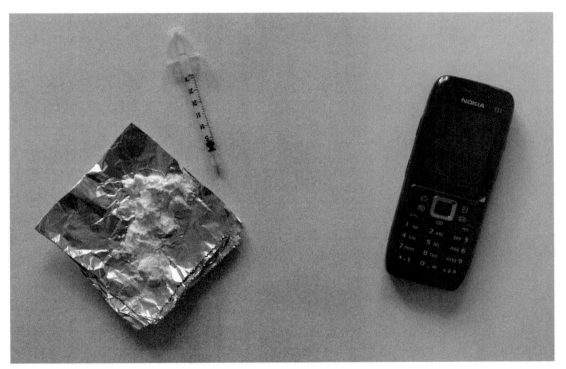

Figure 1.2   Which one of these do you need to get into—and stay in—the music business?

By the way, in case there's any doubt, Figure 1.2 shows an insulin syringe and some flour. Neither the author nor the publisher endorses the use of drugs.

While we can find a few people who fit that description, can I let you in on a secret? That sort of lifestyle was always a myth. More than that, the notion that there was a golden age when it was "easy" to have a career in music is simply untrue. Most importantly, you will also notice that all these tales miss out what happened to the money.

Usually the business was badly organized and everything fell apart, although rather unsurprisingly, while the musicians walked away with nothing, the management and "business" end of the operation always seemed to do all right.

Some people—with a business organization behind them—managed to generate enough income to earn a living as musicians. In contrast, the vast majority of musicians didn't generate *and keep* enough of their income, so they had to get a "proper job" at some point (see Figure 1.3).

Figure 1.3 Is this your idea of a proper job, with prospects? If you don't pay attention to your business, this may be the business you end up working in. © Py2000 I Dreamstime.com

Indeed, even well-respected and highly talented musicians ended up with proper jobs at some point in their career as there was no other way to support their commitments. (In other words, there was usually child support to pay.)

However, that has all changed now.

Reality Check: This Is How You Earn Money Today

There is one true and tested way to have a career in music: Connect with a fan base and then retain that fan base. From that fan base, you must generate your income. That is the whole of it. There is nothing more you need to do in order to live by music alone.

Simply going to the music-related social networking sites (see Figure 1.4) does not help connect *and keep* your fans. Nor does it generate sales. It doesn't matter if you go to one site or 1,000 sites—something else far more important builds that connection between musician and fan. If you don't get what that is, then you ain't going to make money.

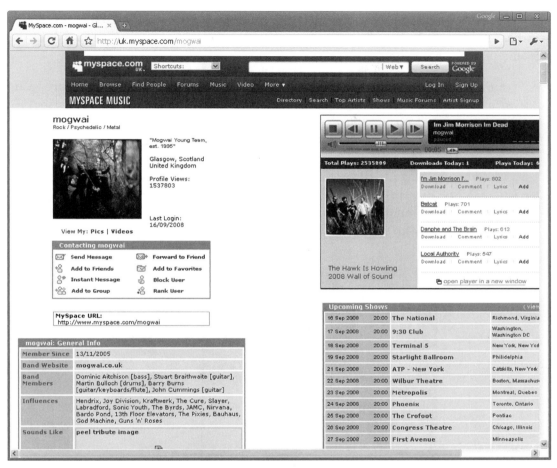

Figure 1.4   The social networking sites may help you get your music out there, but they won't help you keep your fans, and they won't generate income for you.

Equally, if you keep looking back at how people used to make money—and try to follow what people did in the '60s or the '70s—then your chances of success won't be high! The world, and the world beyond music, has changed in the last few years. That is an understatement—the world as we know it has changed beyond all recognition in the last few years. The changes have been social, political, and technological.

The great thing about all this change is that nothing is as it was. The bad thing about all this change is that nothing is as it was.

For the musician and the music business (in the broadest sense), there have been many significant changes over the last few years that have had an impact similar to shifting tectonic plates. These changes include:

- "Youth" culture has changed. There are now far more places where the pre-teen to young adult can spend money. This group of people does not comprise the sole consumers of music, but they do represent the main group. Once, these people had limited options and music was one of the main choices (especially if you wanted to wear a badge of rebellion). But that has now changed, and the people who create and sell products focus great resources on that market. In particular, the markets for computer games, fashion, and communications (cell phones to you and me) have exploded. These industries take money that could have once been directed to music. See Figure 1.5.

Figure 1.5 People would prefer to play with these, rather than go to a gig or buy a CD.
© Norman Chan | Dreamstime.com

- There are fewer venues for live music. People don't care so much about seeing live music (especially when they can stick on a DVD of a good band rather than go to a crummy bar and watch a bad covers band). Sure, stadium rock is still alive and well, but for the people playing computer games and sending text messages to their friends, there are better things to do than follow bands. Applying the rules of supply and demand, a reduction in the outlets for new music means that things get tougher for the performing musician.

- The barriers to entry into the music market are significantly lower. Once you needed to get into a recording studio to make a master-quality recording—the only way a musician could afford that would be if a record label paid. Now every home computer has the power to make recordings that exceed the output quality of studios 10 years ago, and you can even make music on your iPhone (see Figure 1.6). We are now in a situation where anyone (and everyone) can release their material, irrespective of the quality. Again, apply the laws of supply and demand, and make an unhappy face.

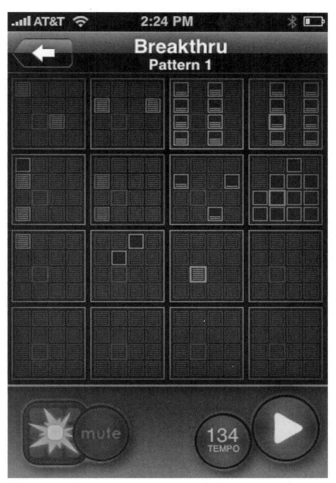

Figure 1.6   You may now make release-quality music on your iPhone or iPod Touch.

■ File sharing and duplication (whether on the internet, by piracy, or through informal sharing) has changed how music is seen and valued. Added to which, there are many musicians who genuinely believe music (especially their own music) should be freely available. File sharing has led to the irony that as the cost of music distribution has been slashed (because it's much cheaper to sell an MP3 file than to sell a CD), the value of music from a consumer's perspective—and the value that a consumer is prepared to pay to get music—has fallen even further.

It has always been tough to earn a living by making music. However, for many reasons—especially the ones noted a moment ago—it is now a lot tougher. Now, that's the downside, and of course there's an upside. The upside is that there are far more opportunities to earn a living from music; you just need to find those opportunities and exploit them. Let me give you a few (very minor) examples:

- With digital distribution, you are no longer limited to selling your music to people in geographical locations where your distributor can get a CD to. Instead, you can now reach everyone around the world who has an internet connection.

- Far more people need music for commercial projects and are willing to pay. For instance, the games market is huge (and still exploding), and the number of television programs (see Figure 1.7) and films that are being made seems to grow hourly.

This book isn't about where you can earn your money: It's about the practicalities of doing business. If you want to read more about the strategies you should be thinking about for developing and exploiting income streams—in other words, the ways you can earn money—then you should check out my book *Building a Successful 21st Century Music Career* (Thomson Course Technology PTR, 2007), which is the companion book to this one. I will refer to this other book at several points. You can read further details about it at noisesculpture.com/c21.html.

What Is Your Business?

So your business is making music, right?

Wrong.

Your business is everything you do (see Figure 1.8). Sure you make music, but is that how you make your money now, and will that be how you continue to make your money? With the new realities, I would suggest that perhaps a modest amount of your money will actually come from making music and quite possibly most of your income will come from the other "stuff" that you sell.

However, your business is not simply about making music—in other words, it's not just about those hours (or however long) that you are on stage or in the studio, or even writing. Your business is about everything you need to do in order to make music and everything you do in connection with making music.

Figure 1.7   This may look like an old television to you. It is—but there are a lot more channels available now than when it was new.

So when you look at your business, you might find that you create income from one or more of the following areas:

- Live performances (gigging).

- Selling CDs/downloads/DVDs and so on.

- Licensing your music to TV/radio or other outlets, such as the internet or games.

Figure 1.8 Part of your music business? It could be... It might help you get to a gig, or it may land you in court if you don't keep it legal. © Constantin Opris I Dreamstime.com

- Commissions: When someone pays you to create some music that could be for a game or a video, or that could be used to commemorate the opening of a shopping mall.

- Mechanical royalties: When your music is reproduced (for instance as a CD).

- Performance royalties: When your music is played on a radio/TV and so on, or in a public place, you should get paid (even if you are not the performer).

- Merchandise (T-shirts and so on).

- Interest/investments: You may have money in the bank or invested elsewhere—this will often be the case if you are holding money for a future expense (such as a tax bill). That income—whether it be interest, dividends, capital gains, or some other form of income—is part of your business.

Mostly your income will come in the form of money (often cash). However, you may also receive payments in kind—for instance, you may get paid in beer or in some other non-cash way (see Figure 1.9). Most musicians won't complain too hard about payment in beer. However, cold, hard cash can be much more appealing. The key issues about non-cash payments are:

- It's still income and needs to be declared as such (for instance to the tax authorities). Ascribing a value to those "earnings" may then be difficult when you complete your tax return and need to share earnings between the musicians.

Figure 1.9   How would you rather be paid? If you do take the beer, then please ensure it is worth far more than the cash equivalent of what you should be paid (as you can be sure that whoever wants to pay you in beer will acquire it at a much lower price than you would pay in a bar).

■ If you are paid in a form that cannot be immediately consumed, then you may need to convert that non-cash payment into cash—that conversion process could then create a whole new (non-music) business for you! The 1970s pop group ABBA earned a considerable amount from the former Soviet Union—as the Soviet currency had little value in the West, the band was paid in oil, which they could then trade on the open market. You may not reach this level, but you should be open to all the ways you can receive income.

Those may be some of the areas where you might earn money; however, you're going to have to do other things too. For instance, take the simple example of a gig—there's a lot of stuff in there, a lot of "moving parts" and a lot of things happening off stage. Here are some examples:

- You need songs. (Otherwise, what are you going to play at the gig?) Whose songs will you play? If you play your own song that you have co-written with your musical collaborators, then who has what rights to each song?

- You need to rehearse. Who will pay for the rehearsal space?

- You need instruments. Who owns the new bass the rest of the band bought because the bass player lost his last one in a nasty divorce?

- How are you getting to the gig? Who is meeting the cost of fuel? As you are getting paid (albeit mostly in beer), your car's insurance company regards this journey as for business purposes—do you have the appropriate insurance? If not, who is liable if you crash?

- Who is paying the sound guy?

- Who is going to sell T-shirts for you? What commission are they taking on sales?

- You're playing five gigs this month—who is figuring out what everyone has earned?

This is just the beginning of the issues you need to contemplate. You will notice that the examples I have chosen all have one thing in common: They're business-related. If you don't deal with the business aspects, then you may:

- Fall out with your collaborators.

- Spend too much money or spend money you don't have.

- Get ripped off and not know it.

- Generate a tax liability (which you may or may not have the money to pay).

- Break the law. (Ignorance really is no excuse when they come to slap the cuffs on.)

- Make yourself liable for the **** ups of one of your fellow musicians.

So *What* Is Your Business?

Okay, that's enough messing around. I presume that as you're reading this book, I don't need to convince you of the necessity to think about business aspects, so shall we try to be a bit more definitive about what your business might include? Here's a more comprehensive list of the possible elements of your business:

- All music-making activities (including writing, rehearsing, recording, and performing)

- All activities in support of music-making activities (for instance, getting to and from a gig)

- Every song you write or co-write (or don't write but perform)

- Every piece of music-making equipment (including the PA/lights and so on)

- All property connected with your music, including the storage space for your gear, any transport, your office, and so on

- All people involved with your business, including fellow musicians, roadies/crew, managers/agents, secretaries/interns/gofers, professional advisers (lawyers, accountants, and so on)

Are you starting to get the idea? Everything, as in *everything*, is your business. If it is about making music or it is something (or someone) that you need in order to make music (or to help), or if it is something (or someone) who helps afterwards, then that is/they are part of your business.

If you want, you can look at it another way—what is not part of your business?

But Why Do *I* Care about All of This Business? I Just Want to Make Music!

While you might have bought into the notion that business is important, can I just labor the point for the moment about why it is important—and why all of the musicians involved in the process should take the business aspects as seriously as they take their music? You never know when you might have to explain to your bass player—for the 367th time—why this stuff is important. Perhaps these thoughts might help to bolster your argument!

Simplistically, the business aspects of your music come down to two things:

- Money

- Power

If you don't deal with the business, then you won't have either of those. You would be surprised how intertwined these two issues are—and how much their influence can corrupt (see Figure 1.10).

Figure 1.10 It's all about money and power, and one often leads to the other, although some people take things to extremes. © Andreea Dobrescu I Dreamstime.com

You may passionately believe that your music should be free and it should be heard. You may make your music available for free download on the internet, and you may play all the free gigs you get invited to play at. Ignoring the basic issue that I'm not sure how you pay for food and put a roof over your head, you would still have to address business issues. Let me give you some examples:

- You want your music to be free, so you give it away on the internet and say, "This is free—it belongs to you." How are you going to feel when someone takes your music, puts it on a CD, and starts selling it? There's nothing to stop them from doing this—you made the business decision that all of the rights to your recording would be given away for free.

- You've just recorded your new CD in a studio you didn't like and with a producer you didn't like. Now you're going on tour to places you don't want to go, in a tour bus you don't like, and you will be staying in hotels you loathe. What happens when you don't like the cover of your new CD, don't like the tracks that were chosen to go on the CD—you know there were much better songs and those that are included aren't finished—and you don't like the marketing campaign created to promote the CD. You said, "I'm all about the music," refused to get involved, and the vacuum you left was filled by fools who don't understand your music. You don't have any say because you refused to engage in the business aspects.

- What do you do when you find that your manager cut your fee in exchange for a gig promoter including another band (coincidentally managed by your manager, too) on the same bill?

- You play a free gig—it's free, so it's free from any contracts, too—and then receive several requests for money. Your roadies want to be paid, the PA company has asked its lawyers to write to you, and a guy who got scalded by hot fat when the burger cart fell over is suing you. What do you do? After all, it was "your" gig.

All of these are issues related to the business. You may not *want* to deal with it, but the business implications of not dealing with these issues may be so profound that if you don't address them, you'll end up without a living.

Business isn't just about the money—although it is a big part of it—it's about everything that happens around you making music. If you don't want to deal with some issues—and as I've said, that is quite reasonable (I mean, who really wants to fill in tax forms?)—then you need to ensure that someone else does. And whoever that person is, you need to trust him or her completely.

The key issue to remember is that while someone else may do something for you, the responsibility still rests with you. Think about a practical example: If you're playing a gig, you can't mix your sound (because you're on stage, not listening to you on stage). So you hire a sound person. If the sound person wrecks the sound, then who are the punters going to blame, you or the sound person? They're going to blame you, and rightly so: You hired the sound person, so it's your responsibility to ensure he can perform his duties correctly. If he can't perform, then fire him.

Your approach should be the same for all aspects of business. It is your responsibility to: (1) take control and (2) make sure things are done (even if all you do is make sure someone else does them for you). The more you understand what needs to be done, the greater will be your ability to find someone to do it, which will leave you with more time to make music.

The Principles of Business

There are some really strange ideas about business out there.

One myth is that "business" gives you a free hand to behave like a complete * * * *. This attitude is often fostered by many of the business-related reality shows on TV, where socially inept fools do unspeakable acts, which they justify under the all-embracing excuse of "that's business."

Can we be clear on a few things? "Business" does not give you the right to forget your humanity. In the name of business, it is not, repeat *not*, acceptable to sell your grandmother (whether whole or for individual body parts), inflict physical cruelty on children and/or animals, or be anything other than absolutely courteous when dealing with strangers.

Indeed, business requires higher standards of the individual. For instance, not only must you be honest, but you must be able to prove you are honest. You are dealing with people with whom you want to build a relationship (your fellow musicians, your fan base, and your business partners, such as gig promoters and the like). You should therefore hold yourself and your behavior to a higher standard.

Most people get into music because it is enjoyable and they have a passion for it. Some people get into business for the same reasons. However, if you got into music, then you probably want to spend your time making music and not dealing with the business side of things.

That is quite understandable and quite an acceptable attitude. However, that is not an excuse to be ignorant of the business aspects or to neglect the business aspects.

So if you're going to set yourself up as a business, what does that mean for your conduct? As a start, I would suggest that in achieving your business goals, you should:

- Comply with the law and with the local practices in your jurisdiction. In order to comply, you need to know what is legal and what is not, and if you are at all unsure, you should take legal advice immediately.

- Be clear in all your dealings. What does that mean in practice? Generally, get it in writing. You think you own the band name and are due 50 percent of the band's income? What do the other seven members of the band think? If you've all signed a band agreement, then these details should be covered. Once you have said you will do something, do it or change the agreement.

- Be smart. Although you will want to behave in an ethical manner, you can still collect all the money that is due to you while minimizing the amount of money you spend. The minimizing part is important—if you get things right the first time, then you will spend a lot less time and money than you would trying to fix the problem at a later date.

Business and Money

The mention of money is the point at which most musicians get squeamish.

However, any money that is around is yours—it doesn't belong to anyone else. As the musician (and writer), you are the person (or people) who are responsible for the creation of the "product" that is then sold. Everyone who makes money all the way down the chain is making money because of you—they are not making money because of anything they have created. They are simply taking a percentage of your earnings.

So don't get squeamish about money, unless you want to be squeamish about how much of your money is being taken by other people.

Breakeven Point

When talking about money, it is important to understand the breakeven point. For any product (whether that be a tangible product, such as a CD, or a more ephemeral product, such as an MP3 download or a gig), there will be a cost associated with the product.

Take the example of a CD. This might have several costs of production, including:

- The studio costs—the studio hire, the cost of the engineers and the producer, and the cost of the crew who were there during the recording

- The cost of production of the CD

- The distribution costs—in other words, the cost of getting the CD into stores

- The cost of keeping your CD in the stores—stores have to pay rent and look after their staff

Although the materials for your CD may be quite cheap, much of the rest of the cost of a CD has to be met from the difference between the cost of manufacture and the selling price. So it might cost (for example) $2 to manufacture the CD, but it may then sell for $10. The $8 difference would go to meeting all of the other costs associated with the CD.

However, there is another issue from a commercial perspective: Most of the costs are upfront. Even if you only look at the studio cost and the cost of manufacturing several thousand CDs, that can still be a considerable expense. Moreover, those costs are fixed.

When you come to sell your CD, you don't pass all of the costs on to the first person who buys a CD. Instead, you spread those costs over all of the people who buy the CD.

If enough people buy the CD, then you make a profit. If they don't, then you take a loss (and if you're not careful, bankruptcy follows, many of your assets get seized, and life becomes fairly tedious).

The breakeven point is the point at which a project moves from a loss to a profit. Let me illustrate this with an example—we'll stay with the CD. Let's say your costs are:

- Recording the CD (including studio, engineer, and producer): $50,000

- Cost to manufacture 25,000 CDs: $50,000

That gives a total cost of $100,000. If you then sell all of your 25,000 CDs at $10, you will earn $250,000, of which your profit will be $150,000. However, that assumes you sell all of your CDs... if you don't, you could have a loss on your hands.

Now take a look at Figure 1.11, which illustrates the breakeven point.

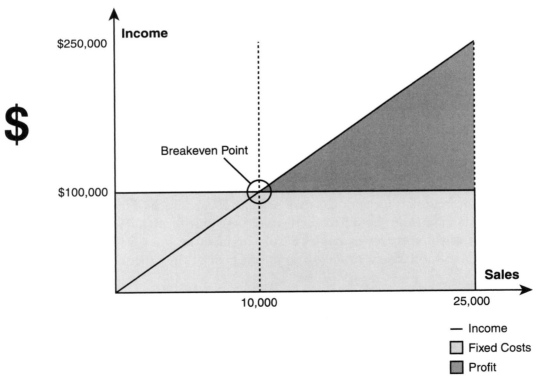

Figure 1.11 The breakeven point.

As you can see, after selling 10,000 CDs you will have generated $100,000, which is equal to the expenses on the project. This is the breakeven point. When you sell your 10,001st CD, then you will move into profit. In this example, having sold 10,001 CDs, the total profit will be $8.

If you're thinking that this looks like a really good profit, it is. These numbers are just for illustration. In practice, there would be a lot more costs and a lot more practical problems in dealing with 25,000 CDs—for instance, storage. Added to which, selling 25,000 CDs is a mammoth task.

Cost and Value

As a creative person, you quite literally create something out of nothing. You create music where there was silence—you create a performance where there was stillness. Not only that, but you create value. When you take your music and add a little bit of plastic in the shape of a disc (something we commonly call a CD), you create something that people will buy.

Now that is incredibly cool! However, it gets better than that. You can create something that:

- Costs less to create than you generate in income

- Is valued more highly by purchasers than the cost to them

Take a CD as an example. Say the manufacturing cost is $2 and you sell it for $10. Each time you sell a CD, you make a profit of $8. So if you're the person who just paid $8 more than it cost to make the CD, you're angry, right? Wrong, you're delighted—you would have been willing to pay $15 or $20 for the CD because it contains your favorite songs. To you, that disk isn't a lump of plastic with a price—it's an invaluable part of you.

Before you read any further, please stop and ponder—this notion is quite profound and may take time to sink in. I should also point out that I didn't invent this idea, so I am in no way laying claim to being a profound individual.

In the next section, I will start looking at how to increase your income (which is always a good thing). Businesses often get squeamish about raising their prices—and I would encourage you not to gouge money out of your fan base—however, it is important to understand the value chain here (see Figure 1.12).

For this to work, the purchaser of your CD (or whatever he buys from you—it could equally be a DVD, a T-shirt, or a gig ticket) must perceive that the value he is receiving exceeds the cost of what he pays. As long as he is doing that, he will keep paying you money.

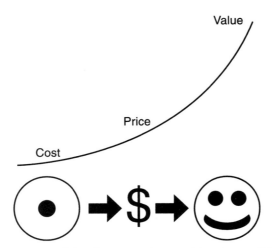

Figure 1.12 You create something for a certain cost. You then sell it for a higher price. The purchaser ascribes a value to his purchase that is higher than the price he paid for your product.

As soon as the purchaser perceives the value of what he is receiving is less than what he paid, then you will lose him. Therefore, you need to ensure that everything that gets to your fans exceeds their hopes and expectations. This means that when they get your next CD, it must be better than the last, and when they come to your next gig, it must be the best gig they have ever been to. You get the idea!

Increasing Your Income

Once you have your fan base, its size determines your income, and that is the limit within which you must live, so you must cut your economic cloth accordingly. If you want to earn more money (and who doesn't?), then you need to:

- Get more money out of each fan, and/or

- Increase the number of people in your fan base

This might sound blisteringly obvious, but if it's not, take a moment to think about it. Your money has to come from somewhere, and if not your fan base, then where will it come from? Now, of course, there are other options (and many of these, such as licensing, are discussed in *Building a Successful 21st Century Music Career*), but fundamentally, your fan base is it.

There is one other option you need to look at: your middle line (see Figure 1.13). Now if you're scratching your head, let me explain. We all understand the bottom line—this

Accounts

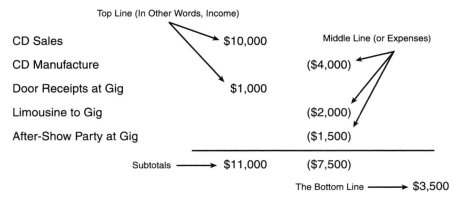

Top Line (In Other Words, Income)

		Middle Line (or Expenses)
CD Sales	$10,000	
CD Manufacture		($4,000)
Door Receipts at Gig	$1,000	
Limousine to Gig		($2,000)
After-Show Party at Gig		($1,500)
Subtotals	$11,000	($7,500)
		The Bottom Line → $3,500

Figure 1.13 Income is often called the top line and expenditure the middle line. In practice, these figures are likely to have their own columns. As you can see, parentheses (brackets) are often used to denote expenses/losses.

notion comes from accounts where the bottom line shows how much has been earned or lost. As a musician, the bottom line may be more practically thought of as your take-home pay (before tax and any other deductions).

Above the bottom line you will find the top line and the middle line (which may actually be a lot of different lines):

- Your top line is your income, or the amount of money you have earned. Clearly, increasing your top line will have an effect on your bottom line.

- Your middle line is your expenses. The less money you spend—for instance, if you take the bus rather than ordering a limousine to take you to the gig—the bigger your bottom line will be. Indeed, if you look back to Figure 1.13, if the limo had been cancelled and the after-show party had also been shelved, the gig could have made a profit.

When you start thinking as a businessperson and not just a musician, you will start looking at how to increase your top line *and* reduce your middle line.

Increasing Your Top Line

So how do you increase your top line? Well, there are several things you can do. As a first step, as I have already mentioned, increase the size of your fan base and increase the income from that fan base. You can increase the income from your fan base by selling them more stuff! For instance, you could:

- Gig more often

- Release a new CD/DVD

- Increase your range of merchandise (add a different color T-shirt or start selling souvenir mugs)

You can also charge more money for everything you do. Charge more for CDs/DVDs, raise the prices of your merchandise, and negotiate higher rates for your gigs (and/or get more people to turn up). This is not an easy thing to do! However, this is business we're dealing with, and sometimes you've got to make tough decisions.

By the way, if you're wondering how much you should charge, look at it another way: How much will people pay? Try pushing your prices up until sales drop (and if you don't like the new levels of sales, you can always drop your prices).

Also, try to focus on profit, not income. So for instance, if it costs you $3 for each T-shirt that you order, then it would be better to sell 100 at $13 than 500 at $5.

That's probably counterintuitive. On the face of it, selling 500 will always be better than selling 100, but let's look at the math:

- If you sell the T-shirts at $5, then you are making $2 profit per shirt ($5 − $3).

- If you sell the T-shirts at $13, then you are making $10 profit per shirt ($13 − $3).

- 500 × $2 profit = $1,000 profit.

- 100 × $10 profit = $1,000 profit.

You're probably wondering why $1,000 profit is better than $1,000 profit. What's the difference? The difference is the effort it takes to sell 500 T-shirts versus 100. Think of the time and effort, the people you need to pay to be at your stall, the cost of storage and transportation, and so on. Taken together, those factors make selling 100 T-shirts a much better financial proposition.

However, there is of course the issue of marketing: Which would you rather have—100 people advertising you on their chest, or 500 people shouting out your name? Sometimes you might find it better to cut the price, deal with the hassle of selling 500 T-shirts, and reap the reward from the publicity.

Which is better for you? I don't know, but when you start thinking like a businessperson, you'll be able to weigh all the options.

Equally, don't increase your numbers if doing so will lead to bigger losses. So if you make a loss when you play gigs, don't play more gigs! It will only lead to bigger losses. Find some way to make the gigs profitable and then play more.

Decreasing Your Middle Line

As well as increasing your income, you should look at decreasing your expenditures. The more you can do to cut this middle line, the greater your overall profits will be.

To start making these savings, you need to be:

- Logical

- Creative

- Hard-headed

The logical part of you needs to think about where you are wasting money. Are you doing too many van journeys—could you do fewer, and would a motel be cheaper than coming home each night? The creative side of you needs to think about things you could do differently. The hard-headed part of you needs to negotiate so you spend less money. For instance, if you hire a van once, you'll probably have to pay whatever price is asked. However, if you hire a van regularly, then you should ask for a discount, and if you don't get it, hire a van from somewhere else.

You need to look for every opportunity to spend less money. Not only that, you need to keep looking for opportunities to spend less money. Just because you got a deal on the van hire, that doesn't mean you can't get a better price in three months' time. Stay aware of the deals that might be out there. Remember, this is business!

Infrastructure and Implementation

Once you have a grip on the concept of what your business actually *is*, then you need to start thinking about the tools that you need to execute the business. There are two things you need to focus on:

- Infrastructure: The tools you need to do your business. These could range from a guitar to play at a gig to a computer to update your website.

- Implementation: How things happen, or more to the point, *who* makes things happen. Who are the people running the business?

Let's look at these issues in a bit more detail.

Infrastructure: Stuff You Need

The tools you will need include:

- Instruments (see Figure 1.14). These are the basic tools of your trade. A plumber will have his or her own tools, and your tools are equally important in undertaking your work.

- Other gear, such as the PA system and the van or other transport to get to gigs.

- Your office. This could be real, virtual, or both. Your office is discussed in greater detail in Chapter 2, "Setting Up Your (Virtual) Office."

- A place to write music and a place to rehearse. You may write alone, in which case you will probably write wherever you are. However, if you collaborate in the writing—especially if you are using amplified instruments as part of this process—then you probably need a dedicated location. When it comes to rehearsing, you will want someplace where all of the musicians can play together. If you don't have your own rehearsal space, then you need to hire somewhere.

- A place to record music. You don't need your own studio, but if you are going to record, then someone needs to book time in a studio somewhere.

Implementation: Making It Happen

In addition to the infrastructure, there are the people who make your business run.

You don't need all of these people—indeed, you don't need these "people," you can split the jobs between the other band members—however, you will probably need to perform all of the following tasks at one point or another. Failure to complete these tasks means that your business will not "happen"—that could mean a missed gig, or it could mean some time in jail for tax evasion.

These key tasks are:

- Manager. You need someone to represent you in your business dealings.

- Gig booker. You need someone to liaise with gig promoters to book gigs—this function may be fulfilled by the manager.

- Administrator. You need someone to look after all those bits of paper and to make sure that things happen.

Figure 1.14   You understand the need for your instrument, but take some time to think about the other tools you will need.

- Roadies. You need crew to make sure your gear is working (and to run the sound/lights and so on while you play).

- Accountant/bookkeeper/auditor. You need people to do the numbers, prepare and audit accounts, and help you with taxes. In practice, your auditor may be separate from any bookkeeper/accountant and will probably be required to have specific professional qualifications and be an active member of a professional body. On a matter of cost, if you hire someone to work as your administrator, you may want them to fulfill the role of bookkeeper, too.

- Lawyer. From time to time you will need a lawyer to advise you on how to comply with the law (for instance, when you set up your business or when you hire people). By definition, if you are seeking the advice of a lawyer, you will want that person to be qualified!

Even the smallest of bands who may be just starting their business will need most, if not all, of these functions under control from the get-go.

How to Set Up a Business

One vexing issue is how to set yourself up as a business. This is vexing for several reasons:

- There are lots of options, and often you will have a choice between options that cannot be readily compared—by the way, these options may vary depending on which jurisdiction you establish your business in.

- You have to deal with complicated and tedious stuff.

- You probably need to get a lawyer and/or an accountant involved at some point.

However, there are a few key questions that will help you figure out which route to take:

- Are you setting up your business on your own or with other people (such as the other members of a band)?

- Do you want your liability to be limited? In other words, if something goes wrong, would you like some legal protection to stop you from losing your house, car, guitar, and all your other worldly possessions?

Now that you've made these important decisions, here are the main options (and as I hinted earlier, these options may not all be available in your jurisdiction—I recommend you check with a local lawyer if you are not sure whether an option is open to you).

Sole Trader (Sometimes Called Sole Proprietor)

A sole trader (or sole proprietor) is the simplest business to establish. You declare that you are a business and that's it. There's no paperwork and there are no legal permissions—you are a business. However, in some jurisdictions, you do need to register as being self-employed.

As the business, you personally receive all of the income and take all of the responsibility. That means if anything goes wrong, you stand to lose everything. Equally, when it comes to employing people, their contract of employment will be directly with you, so if there's a delay in paying their salary, they're likely to turn up at your front door (and I'm guessing they won't be in a good mood if they haven't been paid).

Partnership

A partnership is an agreement by individuals to work together. Instead of individuals transacting business, the partnership undertakes the business, so if you're playing a gig, it is the partnership that agrees to play, not the band members individually.

A partnership can be established by an oral agreement, although to avoid misunderstandings it is usually best to put something in writing—even something quite brief can always be expanded upon. Usually a partnership agreement will set out:

- Each of the partner's interest in the partnership—in other words, what percentage of the partnership's income each person receives.

- What the partnership owns—for instance, the partnership could buy you that new Strat you've always wanted....

- How partners will leave the partnership (when a band member leaves) and how the new band member can join the partnership.

There is a significant downside with partnerships: personal liability. This comes in two forms:

- First the partners have individual unlimited liability (like sole traders). This means that if something goes wrong, all of the partners are equally liable to meet the debt.

- Second, each partner is liable for the other partner's debts. So if your keyboard player orders $50,000 of kit and then gets abducted by aliens, that $50,000 will be recovered from everyone else. Now here's the really nasty bit—the creditor will recover it from whoever they can find. So if the first person they come across just happens to have $50,000 in their bank, the creditor will chase that money. They will not make any effort to apportion the debt between the remaining partners.

If you are working with other musicians and you don't put formal arrangements in place, then in most jurisdictions you are likely to be regarded as working as a partnership. Please don't think this means that you can ignore the necessity to set up a formal partnership—if you don't put proper documentation in place, then statutory provisions will usually apply. These may mean, for instance, if any one member leaves the band, the whole partnership has to be dissolved. In this instance, there would be no partnership to honor existing obligations (so the former partners could get sued for non-fulfillment of their obligations), and you may have to liquidate all of the assets (in other words, sell all the instruments) in order to split the assets of the partnership.

It's important to note that if you are a band, you don't have to make each member a partner automatically. For instance, you may have a nucleus of the band—perhaps the singer, the guitarist, and the keyboard player—who form a partnership. The drummer and the bassist could then work as sole traders and be musicians for hire. The significance of being musicians for hire is that the drummer and the bassist would then be paid a fee rather than sharing in the partnership's profits. The drummer and bassist would also avoid a share of any liability that falls on the partnership (as they would not be partners).

Limited Liability Partnership

Unlimited liability can be quite scary—and it can do huge damage. If you like the idea of a partnership, but you want to keep your house, then you might like the idea of a limited liability partnership.

As the name suggests, this is a partnership in which the liability of the partnership is limited. Generally, in return for this protection, the partnership will be subject to greater legal or regulatory scrutiny. (In other words, you could find that the partnership has to get crawled over for longer by auditors and that you have to fill in more governmental forms.)

Corporation (with Limited Liability)

Before limited liability partnerships, and in jurisdictions where these partnerships aren't allowed, the only way to limit liability was to establish a corporate structure—in other words, to form a company.

Companies were originally established so that people could invest money in a business but limit their liability to the amount they had invested. This meant that if a business failed, then the creditors of the business couldn't chase the investors for their debts. Without this legal protection, investors were reluctant to put money into businesses.

The flipside to this protection is greater disclosure, and in most jurisdictions companies are required to undergo an annual audit and must then make their audited accounts and other details about the company publicly available.

With partnerships, the partners run the business. By contrast—and to reflect their origins as a way to protect investors—companies are run by a board of directors who are accountable to the investors (who are called *shareholders*). An investor can also be a director but does not need to be, so you could establish your business as a company and appoint someone else as a director to run things.

With a partnership, all of the partners take a share of the profits and share the losses. With a company:

- The losses remain within the company. There is no necessity for the shareholders to take a share of the losses; however, they could lose all of the capital they invest in the business.

- Shareholders get paid in two ways:
  - First, if they act as employees, then they will receive a salary.
  - Second, the directors pay out the profit (after retaining an amount to meet future expenses and possible losses) as dividends.

With a company, if you choose to be a director, then you will be treated as an employee for tax purposes. Generally, this means that there is a stricter application of the tax laws and you would not be able to offset business expenses. While this may not sound encouraging, it is balanced by the fact that the company can offset these expenses, so there may not be any overall tax gain or loss.

Doing Business As

Doing business as… isn't a different legal structure; however, in several jurisdictions there is a legal requirement to register if you are doing business as anything other than your legal name. So if you are a partnership and that partnership doesn't reflect the name you do business as (for instance, if your partnership name does not reflect the band's name), then you need to get registered (swiftly).

Other Liability Issues

Just because you establish yourself as a business with limited liability, that does not mean you will never have liability.

Limited liability cannot take away your personal liability for your own acts. This means that if you can be pursued for any liabilities you may have (or any liabilities that may be attributed to you, which may happen if someone wants to sue you for a really large amount of money). Although this may seem like a downside, there is no legal way to protect against your own stupidity. Equally, limited liability will not limit your liability with respect to criminal acts.

One step you can take—and indeed will be required to take in certain areas—is to arrange insurance. For many of your activities, you will be required to have insurance—for instance:

- Any car or van will need insurance (and in the case of a privately owned vehicle, this insurance will need to extend to business purposes since driving to and from a gig or recording session constitutes business—worse still, you may have to declare that business is as a musician, which may raise your premiums).

- You will be required to carry public liability insurance for certain events, and the insurance you are likely to be required to carry may cover liabilities of several million dollars.

You should seek advice from a reputable insurance broker who will be able to advise you about the insurance you are required to carry in your jurisdiction.

However, even with limited liability and insurance, that doesn't mean you won't be at risk of litigation. As your business reaches a level at which people may perceive that you have money—even if you don't—you may want to carry out some sort of risk assessment to identify whether you have any potential liabilities.

Some of these risks may be easy to identify—these risks should be addressed immediately. Other risks may be nearly impossible to foresee. For instance, a few years ago the rock band Judas Priest—or rather, the individual members of the band along with their record label—were sued for an alleged subliminal message embedded in one of their tracks, which, it was alleged, led to one of their fans committing suicide. This message could only be accessed by playing the track backwards (which was not easy as this was at a time when albums came out on vinyl, and "scratching" wasn't common in the rock community).

Although the members of the band and the label won, this was only after a trial. The consequences for the individuals if they had lost would have been disastrous.

Location, Location, Location

Before we go too much further, I would like to stress two points:

- This book does not constitute legal advice.

- Legislation differs depending on your jurisdiction—so legislation will be different for different states and different countries.

Before you take any action, please ensure that you understand which legislation applies to you. If you are a band based in New York state, then New York state law and U.S. federal law will apply to you. However, if you get offered a gig in Canada and you go over the border to play that gig, then Canadian law will apply to you while you are in Canada.

This may seem self-evident, and to be frank, the differences between the U.S. and Canadian law are unlikely to be huge. However, there are issues that may be significant when you cross borders. In particular:

- Tax regimes will be different. As well as the obvious different applications of different tax legislation, the registration and notification requirements differ between jurisdictions, so you should check whether there is any time limit on registering for tax purposes after you have established your business.

- Your personal liability may be different, and measures put in place to limit your liability in one country may not apply in another.

- Your insurance coverage may not apply, so if you drive from New York to Canada, you may find that as you cross the border, that really good, but really cheap, insurance policy on your van has just run out, and more than that, your public liability insurance doesn't cover you either.

If you are serious about your business, then seek appropriate professional advice from someone qualified to give advice in each and every jurisdiction in which you will be operating.

Is that enough warning? Good! Let's get on with the book.

2 Setting Up Your (Virtual) Office

Your office is the nerve center of your music business. It is the place from which all of your business is undertaken, and it is also where all of your information is collected in one place—details about your financial arrangements are stored, gigs are booked, contracts are retained (see Figure 2.1).

The point of having an office is so that all of the information is there—you can access it immediately and act upon it. For instance, if someone offers you a gig on November 13, can you take it? This decision will be based on a number of factors. If you are already booked, then you probably can't do the gig. If the gig is in Florida and you are in Tokyo on the previous day, then I'm guessing there may be logistical challenges in making the gig. If you can't immediately access your schedule, then you're likely to have problems deciding whether you can make the gig.

Alternatively, if the tax authorities say you owe them an amount equivalent to two years' income, what do you do? If you have records of your income and copies of all of the correspondence with the authorities, then you will be able to show that there has been a misunderstanding (assuming the debt does not relate to any unpaid amounts).

As a third scenario, suppose your new T-shirts turn up and proclaim "World Tour 2003," which is rather upsetting if it's 2008. If you can immediately find your instructions to the T-shirt manufacturer and show that the error is on their part, then you might be able to get a new run of T-shirts before the tour starts. If you don't have immediate access to your instructions, then you may have difficulty negotiating a change.

Perhaps the most important step for running a music career as a business is to set up the office. However, your office doesn't need to be a conventional office like the ones that your parents may work in (see Figure 2.2). You're a musician—you don't do business in one place, so your office should be wherever you are as far as possible. Not only does it need to be in several places, but it may need to be in several places at once—you may

Figure 2.1 Some of the things your office might need to handle.

need to deal with something while you're on the road, and you may have someone back at base who needs to work in the office, too. This used to be a challenge, but now it's quite easy to manage, and technology has brought us into the age of the virtual office.

In the 21st century, you can run most of your business pretty much from anywhere you can access a computer (or PDA/Smartphone).

When Physical Location Is Important

Although you may be able to have a virtual location anywhere in the world, there are times when you will need a set physical location, for legal reasons and sometimes for practical reasons. Here are a few examples:

- All businesses need a location where legal notices (whether from the government or as part of court proceedings) may be served upon them. When you register your business, you will find that giving the business address as "I am where I am, man, so don't push it" won't go over very well.

- You may also find it convenient to have a place to which all other paperwork (such as invoices and bank statements) is directed. Clearly, you could use a post office box address, but even then the paperwork needs to reach a physical location at some point, and carrying every piece of correspondence you have ever received while you are on the road is not practical (assuming you can organize the postal redirection).

- To the extent that you have paperwork or other documentation—in particular, documentation that you may be required to keep, perhaps for tax purposes—you

Figure 2.2   Is this what you think of when you think about an office, with lots of people wearing nasty suits and running around doing lots of things that they don't really understand or care about? © Laurent Dambies | Dreamstime.com

will need a location for these documents. You don't need much to store documents, just somewhere safe and secure. So you could use a garage at a family member's house (provided your papers are secure from fire, theft, and natural disasters), or you could rent some storage space. The possibilities are endless, as Figure 2.3 illustrates.

Figure 2.3 Perhaps the garden shed would be a good place to put your office. It doesn't matter how battered the place looks, as long as it is secure and comfortable.

■ If you hire someone to run a part of your business—for instance, you may have someone who responds to your letters and answers your phone—then that person may need a desk to sit at, and that desk may need a place to go.

Choosing the Right Tools—But First...

Setting up an office is not simply about finding some real estate where you can locate your office. However, that may be an issue, particularly if you need to hire someone. Of much greater importance than the geography are the tools that you need, but before you get the tools, take some time to think about the tasks you need to accomplish. You need a shovel only if you're going to go digging—you don't need a shovel if you want to bang nails in (unless you're very odd). You probably want to take a similar approach with your office.

By the same token, don't get too wrapped up in looking for every last conceivable tool you might ever want or need—deal with the key priorities and don't sweat the details. You need to make sure you have the tools that are right for you and that you and your co-workers/collaborators/staff and so on are happy using. As Figure 2.4 shows, you're going to have a lot of issues you want to address, and not all of them will be important.

Figure 2.4   When you set up your office, you need to start thinking about the things that actually matter.

So what tools do you need? That depends on what you're trying to do. Clearly, if you want to write a letter, you need some paper and either a typewriter or a computer (with software loaded and a printer). But you will also need somewhere to rest your computer/typewriter (because trying to work on the floor will get quite uncomfortable after a while).

The choice between a computer and typewriter goes further than whether you are happy with new or old technology and highlights another issue: hardware and software. Some of what you need is hardware and some is software, and as I've already discussed and will discuss further in this chapter, there is the challenge of taking your office with you when you are away from home.

So before we go any further, let's look at what we need to do and figure out some of the tools we might need.

Basics
Before we go any further, I'm assuming you will have figured out:

- Where to locate your office.

- What furniture you need (desks/tables/chairs and so on).

- How to get a phone. Having a separate phone line is pretty much the definition of a business!

Physical Storage

You are going to need to store things, and the main things your business will need to store are pieces of paper. These pieces of paper will cover many things:

- Contracts (both relating to the music and employment contracts) and instructions (for instance, orders)

- Receipts and invoices

- Correspondence, which could include letters from fans or details of the tour you are trying to set up

Although people have been talking about the paperless office for years, even with the best will in the world it is easy to kill several forests running an office. All offices have some paper (it's a matter of lore that cannot be changed, so don't fight it), and your business will be no different.

You will need a way to store all the bits of paper you accumulate—you will probably find that putting each piece of paper into a single folder (see Figure 2.5) doesn't keep pace with your filing requirements, so you will need something sturdier (maybe a filing

Figure 2.5 Envelope wallets may be useful for keeping your papers in order, but you're probably going to need a more sophisticated filing system.

cabinet). Ideally, this storage should keep the papers in some sort of logical order (so you can find the paper at a later date—and if you can't find it, why are you keeping it?) and should protect your records against:

- Theft

- Unauthorized access

- Fire (see Figure 2.6)

- Flood

- Any other disaster or destructive action (manmade or otherwise)

Figure 2.6 If this happened to your business, would you be able to carry on as normal the next day? While the events that befall your business may not be this dramatic, you should be ready for all eventualities.

One option for paper storage is to scan the document and store it electronically. This may be a practical long-term option, but in the short term there may be challenges. First, you have to store the piece of paper long enough for it to be scanned and for that scan to be verified. Second, some agencies do not accept scans of documents. Before you destroy the original document, you should verify that a scan will be acceptable to the courts and other authorities in your jurisdiction—in particular, the tax authorities. Otherwise, if your business is audited, you may have challenges if they don't accept scans and your original records have been shredded.

Another issue to consider is how long you wish to store a document. Many businesses routinely destroy their documents once they no longer have a statutory requirement to keep them. (This statutory period is usually six years or thereabouts, depending on your jurisdiction.) There are two key reasons for this destruction:

- First, space. Documents take up a lot of storage space, and for many corporations the logistics of keeping these bits of paper are tiresome and expensive.

- Second, risk. Many companies take the attitude that whether what they did in the past was right or wrong, they don't care—if they destroy the documents, then they can be assured that there will be nothing within those documents that can harm them at a later date. If the documents are gone, then they're gone. If they are retained—even if there is no legal requirement to retain the documents— then they will always be available to be subpoenaed. (In other words, the company may have to produce the document as evidence against itself in legal proceedings.)

You may also have other physical storage requirements—in particular, if you receive payments (either as cash or checks), then these will need to be stored somewhere safe and secure. Even if you make daily runs to the bank, you may still want to make sure that all monies are (literally) kept under lock and key—especially if your office is readily accessible to the public.

Electronic Storage

I briefly touched on the notion of electronic storage. As well as physical storage, you will need electronic storage. Clearly, if you are creating a document (or similar) on a computer, this will need to be stored somewhere, and that somewhere is conventionally on the computer's hard drive (see Figure 2.7). However, this may not always be the most sensible choice because:

- Hard drives are mechanical devices, and over the longer term, *all* mechanical devices fail at some point. All you have to do is figure out when your drive is going to fail and copy all the crucial documents before then.

Figure 2.7 Hard drives: great while they work—tiresome, and potentially business threatening, when they fail.

- Hard drives fill up. As they get full, their performance degrades, and once there is no more space, then what do you do?

- Files on one computer cannot be readily accessed by someone using a different computer. This is good from a security perspective, but may be inconvenient from a sharing perspective (for instance, if you want to allow your auditor to access your records).

- Getting a new computer will usually necessitate transferring all of the data from your old machine to the new one.

There are several ways to address these challenges, which include:

- Network file storage—in other words, storing your files on a separate machine that is dedicated to storing (electronic) files. These machines usually:
  - Have much larger file capacities.
  - Include mechanisms to protect against disk failure (for instance, by running more than one disk so if one fails the data is still secure).

- Allow access by more than one person. Indeed, some machines can be set up to allow access from any internet connection.

- Online file backup—in other words, copying your files to an online storage service (usually through a specialized piece of software running automatically).

- Cloud computing. For storage purposes, this is like a cross between the first two options, and the data is stored online. Clearly, there may be challenges with this approach, which I will discuss later in this chapter.

From both practical and realistic perspectives, there is no single answer to the challenge of electronic storage, and you may well find that you are using several options.

The Written Word

You are going to need to put many things in writing, for instance:

- Contracts—with employees, with studios, with business partners, with gig promoters, and so on

- Web text and blogs

- Letters

- Press releases

- Text to accompany your CD/DVD and so on

- Lyrics (whether you want to remember the song or you need to record it for copyright purposes)

When you start to think about it, you will probably find that there is no aspect of your business that doesn't need to be put in writing at some point or another.

As you can see, whatever you write could be used in many different ways—each option could suggest a different form of writing tool. The main tools would likely be:

- Word processing software, such as Microsoft Word (see Figure 2.8), which could be used for letters, contracts, and lyrics. Equally, you might want to do a first draft of something before you post it on a social networking site, such as MySpace.

- An HTML editor (or other web creation tools), which could help create (or convert) your words into a format that is suitable for the web.

- A specialist weblog editor (if neither your word processor nor your HTML editor is up to the task); see Figure 2.9.

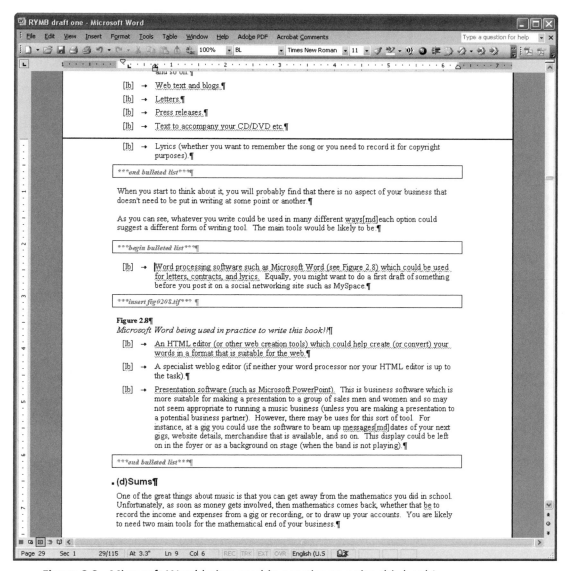

Figure 2.8   Microsoft Word being used in practice to write this book!

- Presentation software (such as Microsoft PowerPoint; see Figure 2.10). This is business software that is more suitable for making a presentation to a group of salesmen and saleswomen and so may not seem appropriate for running a music business (unless you are making a presentation to a potential business partner). However, there may be uses for this sort of tool. For instance, at a gig you could use the software to beam up messages—dates of your next gigs, website details,

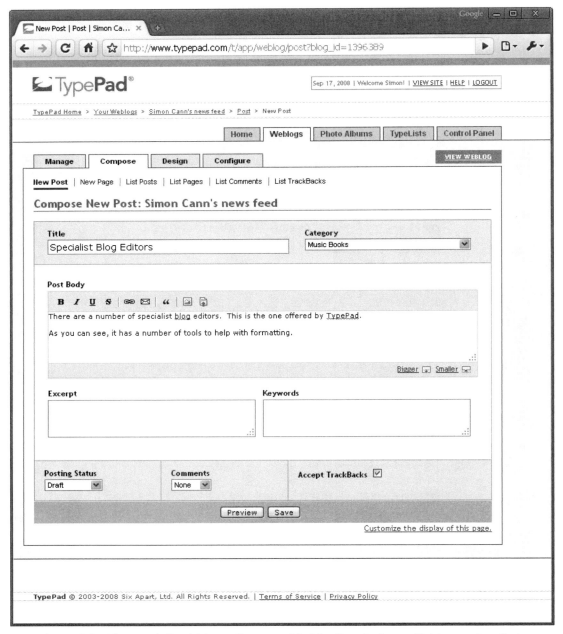

Figure 2.9   The specialized blog editor provided by TypePad to edit blogs using their system.

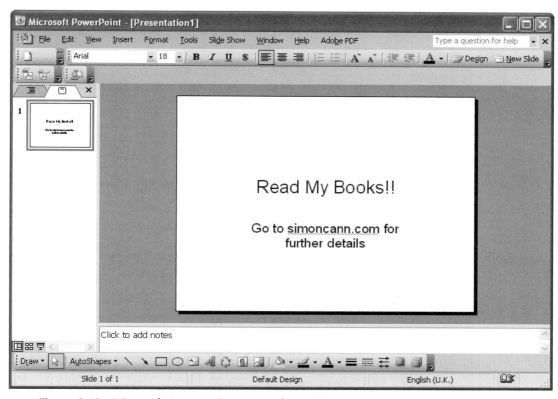

Figure 2.10   Microsoft PowerPoint—great for grabbing some extra publicity!

merchandise that is available, and so on. This display could be left on in the foyer or as a background on stage (when the band is not playing).

Sums

One of the great things about music is that you can get away from the mathematics you did in school. Unfortunately, as soon as money gets involved, then mathematics comes back, whether to record the income and expenses from a gig or recording or to draw up your accounts. You are likely to need two main tools for the mathematical end of your business:

- A spreadsheet, such as Microsoft Excel (see Figure 2.11), which can be used for day-to-day matters, such as keeping tabs on your income and expenditures.

- A specialized accounting package in order to create your accounts. You may get by with a spreadsheet package, but once you reach a certain level, proper accounts are necessary, and it may be wise to invest in a good accounting package. You will often find that you can supply your auditor with accounts in a form that he or

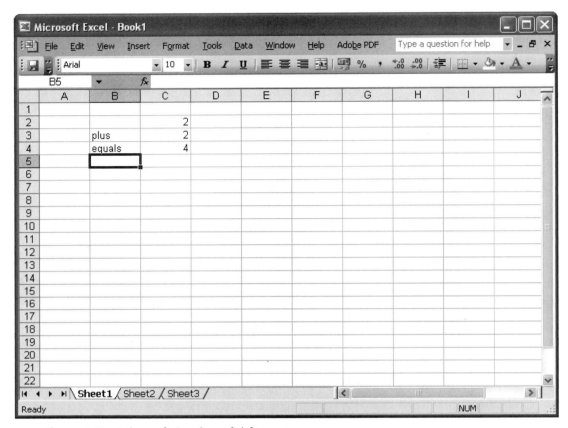

Figure 2.11 Microsoft Excel: useful for sums.

she can analzye very easily if you use a package that is compatible with theirs. Check with your auditor before you make an investment, because you could save yourself a lot of money in professional fees.

Coordination

One thing a music business needs is coordination—the band needs to be in a certain place at a certain time. If you are not there, then you will miss the gig, TV performance, or whatever. And very often, it is not simply a case of getting one person from point A to point B.

Instead, you may have to get the musicians from point A, to an interview in a TV studio, to a meet and greet with some fans, and then on to the airport where they will fly to the next city, meet the concert promoter and a new bunch of fans at another meet and greet, sign a new record-company contract, and then get to the gig at point B, having forgotten to go to bed. Meanwhile, the crew and the equipment may be going from point A to point B on the road, having crossed three international borders and driven hundreds of miles.

The fans at the second gig don't care about the logistical problems—they don't care if customs searched the van 15 times, they don't care if you forgot the drums, they don't care that the singer is tired—they just want what they have paid for: a great show.

If you're reading this book, you may not be working on this scale—yet—however, you could need a lot of coordination. All of the musicians need to know when they are busy (so gigs aren't double booked), and someone needs to know when the band is free so that a gig can be booked. Equally, people need to know where the band will be at any time—you may know that you are free on December 17, but if you're 3,000 miles away on December 16, then you may not be able to get to the gig that someone slipped onto your schedule at the last moment.

Then there's the flip side: Your fans want to know when and where you are playing.

Luckily, there are tools to help people with this sort of coordination—they're called calendars. You will need several! One for each musician, one for the band, and maybe one that can be made public (so that fans will know when and where you are). You can buy lots of paper calendars, but you will probably find that electronic ones are far more convenient.

Choosing the Right Tools

Although I've mentioned a few tools, you will see that I haven't looked at the advantages and disadvantages. Later in this chapter, I will look at some of the tools you could choose. However, before we get there, let's look at some more of the practical issues, in particular:

- Some of the hardware that you will need and also how you can use your existing hardware. If you have an iPhone, you can pretty much already run your music business on the road. Whether that is desirable or whether there are better options, only you can decide.

- Some of the software options—in particular, the different forms of software. There are many new pieces of software that you can use online, and some of these are really good.

- The options and practicalities for sharing your information (within your business and with your fan base).

- Security (both in terms of making sure that only authorized people can see your sensitive data and in making sure you have backups if you lose everything in a fire).

Hardware: What Tool Will You Use to Do Your Work?

Although we live in a software-dominated world, that software still needs hardware: All the latest, greatest, and whizziest online toys need you to be able to get online, which requires some sort of computer.

When you come to do your work or to access your data, you have a number of hardware choices. Each choice has advantages and disadvantages. This section sets out your main options. You will probably find that you want more than one option so you can use the most appropriate hardware in any given location, and so a combination of hardware may be right for you.

Desktop

A desktop computer is your standard office machine—this is a (usually gray) box (see Figure 2.12) with a separate monitor and keyboard. You can also easily add on a printer.

Figure 2.12   If you're anything like normal people, you'll probably try to lose your computer box by fitting it into a convenient gap on the floor.

Desktop computers come in Windows, Mac, and Linux flavors depending on your preferences and your purse. For the purposes of this book, the three flavors are virtually identical in terms of available functionality.

The benefits of this type of computer are:

- Power. You will usually have the most powerful chips available for desktop models, and generally you can get more memory and larger hard disks for these models.

- Price. Generally prices are quite reasonable—usually you will find when you look at the power-to-price ratio that these give the best deal.

- Ease of repair. These boxes are usually easy to open up and contain mostly standard parts that can be easily replaced. Equally, if you break something trivial (for instance, if you spill tea on your keyboard—not very rock and roll, but I can speak from experience), then all you need to do (if you take milk and sugar in your tea) is buy a new keyboard. With a laptop you may need a whole new machine or expensive repairs.

The downside of these models (apart from their ugliness) is that they are not very portable. Generally, you would expect to put them in one place and leave them there (where they will suck in dust, as Figure 2.12 shows). Theoretically, you could take one of these machines on the road, but they may be somewhat fragile, and there are more practical options.

Laptop

Laptops (see Figure 2.13) come in several sizes—from reasonable to rather bulky—but are usually all the same basic shape with a lidded screen that folds over a keyboard. The benefits of laptops are:

- Portability. These computers are much easier to take on the road than a desktop, and they can usually take a bit more shaking than a desktop can.

- Power. Laptops are usually sufficiently powerful (in terms of processor grunt, memory, and hard disk) to be able to run most standard business applications. However, they are usually not quite as powerful as the most up-to-date desktop models.

The downsides of laptops are:

- Battery life. This means that although the laptop may be portable, you also need to take a power supply, which makes them less attractive on the road.

Figure 2.13 A laptop computer with its power supply. It may not be pretty, but it is much easier to transport than a desktop model.

- Fragility. These things are nowhere near as fragile as a desktop; however, it is still quite easy to break a laptop—in particular, they do not respond well to liquids, dropping, and extreme temperatures.

- Internet connectivity. Often you need to connect these to the internet with a piece of wire or be within range of a WiFi hotspot (which may not be close). Alternatively, some laptops can connect to the net through a cell phone (in which case, why not use the cell phone on its own?).

- Theft/loss. You cannot put a laptop in your pocket or your purse. This means the laptop has to be carried externally and so is quite vulnerable to theft. Also, if you're one of those people who loses thing easily, then a laptop is something that may separate itself from you.

Ultra Portable

The dividing line between a laptop and an ultra-portable machine is often quite blurred. Equally, the dividing line between a PDA (described in the next section) and an ultra portable can be quite blurred at times. For the purpose of this book, I will categorize something as being an ultra portable when:

- It has a keyboard, but that keyboard has keys that are smaller than normal, and...

- Its processing power is considerably less than a normal laptop's power.

Very often, but not always, these machines will run specialized software (often a Linux derivative); however, they can also run Windows (albeit slowly). A great example of an ultra portable is the ASUS Eee (see Figure 2.14).

Figure 2.14   The ASUS Eee: a true ultra portable that is capable of being used to run your music business while you're on the road. (For size comparison, this has been placed on top of the laptop used in Figure 2.13—as you can see it is a lot more portable.) This machine comes with a lot of software preinstalled, including Firefox (web browser), Thunderbird (email client), and Open Office Suite (a suite of programs that has functionality similar to Word, Excel, and PowerPoint).

The advantages of these machines are:

- Size. They are small enough to carry easily (and they can usually be packed more discreetly than a laptop, reducing the chances of theft).

- Price. These machines are often much cheaper than a laptop (but they are often less powerful). However, very often the range of software included is surprisingly good, making the value proposition more compelling.

- Battery consumption. These machines are less powerful than the regular laptops (which is not surprising given their price). However, the bundled software may make fewer demands on the processor, meaning that the battery power lasts longer.

- Ruggedness. These machines tend to be more rugged. For instance, the ASUS Eee (shown in Figure 2.14) has a solid-state hard drive. The disadvantage of this is its modest capacity, but this is far outweighed by the benefit of the ruggedness—there are no moving parts to break, which is a great advantage for a machine that you carry with you on the road.

The disadvantages of these machines are:

- Power. While ultra portables often have a much longer battery life than a laptop, they do still run out of juice, meaning that you will have to take a power supply with you. However, you will probably take it out less often than for a laptop.

- Cramped. These machines have small keyboards and small screens, meaning they can be tiresome to work on for long periods—they are certainly not as easy to use as a desktop or laptop.

PDA/Cell Phone

There is a huge range of choice in the PDA (personal digital assistant—PalmPilot) and cell phone market. With these devices you usually get:

- Internet access (sometimes only by WiFi in the case of a PDA).

- Email of some variety (although the web-based mail may be more appealing).

- Limited access to documents. Some will allow you to access and edit documents, some will allow you to view documents, and the really cheap tools won't allow much!

While PDAs and cell phones (see Figure 2.15) may not be ideal devices for web surfing, they can be great if you want to check and send a few emails or write a brief blog post

Figure 2.15 An iPod Touch, a PalmPilot, and a Smartphone—all three could be used to run your music business.

while you are away from home. Most importantly, these devices can live in your pocket, which will greatly reduce the chances of theft or misplacement.

Internet Café

If all else fails, you can always run your business from an internet café (see Figure 2.16).

Clearly this is not an ideal situation, but you may find little choice—for instance, if your laptop is stolen and your cell phone doesn't have coverage in your current area.

Figure 2.16   An internet café can offer many useful facilities to help run your business when you are away from base. © Pavel Losevsky | Dreamstime.com

Cloud Computing: What Is It and Why Does It Matter?

Cloud computing has been around in several forms for a while. It is only recently that it has (1) gotten a name and (2) become the "next big thing."

So what is it, why does it matter so much, and why am I bringing it up here? In short, cloud computing means that you do not need to be tied to a particular piece of hardware, a particular piece of software, or a particular location. Therefore, for many musicians trying to run their music business, cloud computing is the perfect solution because you can access your business from anywhere and everywhere. However, getting cloud computing up and running may take a moment or two!

Anyway, before we move on, let's look at cloud computing in a bit more detail.

Cloud Computing: What Is It?

Cloud computing is a term that is used in many different ways, so it can be quite a difficult concept to grasp. At its most basic, cloud computing is computing where the hard work—in other words, the computer processing and/or the data storage—is done on a remote location (in other words, the data is not stored on the machine on which the person is working). Typically, the cloud service is provided over the internet, so the process will be done at the other end of an internet connection.

A common example of cloud computing is web-based email (see Figure 2.17), which is offered by Yahoo! and Google, among others. So, you have probably already used a cloud service without realizing it.

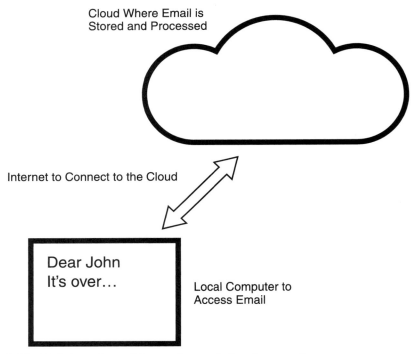

Figure 2.17   Web-based email is one form of cloud computing.

However, in addition to email, there are many other cloud services available these days. Here are a few examples:

- Storage. Files of any sort—including documents, spreadsheets, photos, video files, and so on—can be stored and retrieved from the cloud.

- Sharing. The photo-sharing sites, such as Flickr (flickr.com) are examples of another form of cloud service.

- Calendar/diary tools.

- Internet browser favorites/bookmarks synchronization.

- Task lists management.

- Documents/spreadsheets/presentations. In other words, instead of using Word/Excel/PowerPoint and so on, you can create, edit, and store your document in the cloud.

The key issue to understand is that cloud computing is not an all-or-nothing choice. You could choose to put only part of your business into the cloud—for instance, you could use web-based email and online file storage while you retain (and continue to use) your existing Microsoft Office software. However, as I have already hinted, the cloud offers some significant advantages for the musician on the move who is trying to run his or her business.

Why Is This Different? Why Is This a Step Forward?

There are several key differences between cloud computing and regular computing (where the data is processed on the user's computer and files may be stored on the same computer or on a local network).

The key differences are:

- Someone else looks after the data. It will (usually) be stored on an industrial-strength server (often in several geographic locations on more than one continent), and the appropriate security backups are automatically made. Generally, cloud providers will have much better infrastructure and processes in place to protect your data than you could ever hope to implement.

- There is no need to install a copy of Word, Excel, and an email program on each computer. Instead, all of the functions can be accessed through an internet browser (such as Chrome, Internet Explorer, or Firefox). However, some more advanced cloud functions may require specialized software.

- Someone else manages the software. Any problems with the software are sorted out by the cloud provider. New features can be added without the need to install new software on each computer that accesses the software. Added to which, there is a greatly reduced risk that the user will be able to "break" the software.

Although it is different, cloud computing also brings many new options, a lot of which will appeal to musicians who are not tied to one location. For instance:

- People can access their "office" from anywhere in the world. For instance, as well as accessing your emails online, you could also update a letter and change a spreadsheet from anywhere in the world.

- Data can be accessed in different ways. For instance, emails can be checked on cell phones (in addition to being accessible on a normal computer).

- A centralized address book can be shared between everyone connected with the business.

- Files can be synchronized between several computers (and synchronization with PDAs, such as PalmPilots, can be effected more easily). Indeed, with the cloud, there may not be a need to synchronize data—this is discussed in the next subsection ("To Synchronize or Not to Synchronize").

- Data can be shared. For instance, calendars can be shared, and more than one person can be working on a document at one time. A great example of a sharing cloud service would be a shared calendar—by sharing a calendar of your forthcoming gigs, you can ensure that all of your fans have a ready method to check when you are next playing near them.

- The price is very low—indeed, many providers offer these services for free, and in most cases, the free services will achieve everything you need.

- Equally, the computers that are necessary to do business do not need to be as powerful. This could mean that you could run your business on comparatively low-powered machines, and there would be less need to keep updating the hardware to run the latest software.

- There is also the advantage that you don't need specialized hardware. You would not need a specialized file server to securely store your file, and you would not need an email server to run your email software. Instead, you would just need an internet connection.

- Another cost savings would be the reduction in IT consulting staff. Because the whole process is handled in the cloud, you wouldn't need to call on specialized staff to help you set up your business infrastructure.

- Viruses are less of an issue with the cloud. Your data is held on external networks where the cloud provider will take care of viruses (because if they don't, then their whole business could go down the tubes). This isn't to suggest that you don't need to be cautious about your machine—no one wants their computer to become a spambot or zombie—but the results of catching a virus are likely to be far less damaging for your data.

- You can expand and contract your business very easily. If you hire staff, all they need is a computer with an internet connection and that's it—there is no other significant infrastructure implication to hiring new people.

To Synchronize or Not to Synchronize

The smart ones among you will have noticed a potential flaw in the notion of cloud computing: You are reliant on your internet connection. To an extent you are; however, many of the cloud services now include features that allow you to work offline and fix things when you go back online. However, these can lead to other issues, so let's look at the options. I should also point out that the terms used here and the concepts described are not mutually exclusive.

Single Data Source

With a single data source, you are dealing with data located in one place (even if that data is then backed up). In other words, all of your data is "out there" in the cloud (see Figure 2.18). So for instance, when you open a document, you are editing a file that is stored on the cloud.

The key advantage of the single data source is that there is no confusion—there is only ever one version of a document. Whoever accesses a document and however they access it, they will only ever access the most recent file, so you won't get problems with people sending out data that isn't up to date.

Data Retrieval

Data retrieval is the antithesis of cloud computing in many ways (see Figure 2.19). What happens is that the data is held in the ether, and then software on a local machine copies the data to the local machine and in the process will often delete the data, making it inaccessible to anyone else. This typically happens with email when it is retrieved using a POP (*Post Office Protocol*) process.

Although there are obvious drawbacks relating to sharing and accessibility, there are significant advantages to this approach:

- The data will all be stored in one place—the local machine to which the data is retrieved.

- Data is deleted from the cloud, reducing the risk of unauthorized access.

- You won't pay to store unwanted data in the cloud.

Synchronization

With synchronization, there is a local copy of the data and a cloud copy of the data. When synchronization occurs, the two versions of the data are compared (see Figure 2.20). If one data source has a newer file than the other, then the older file is overwritten with the new. This comparison is undertaken on a file-by-file basis until the two data sources are in sync.

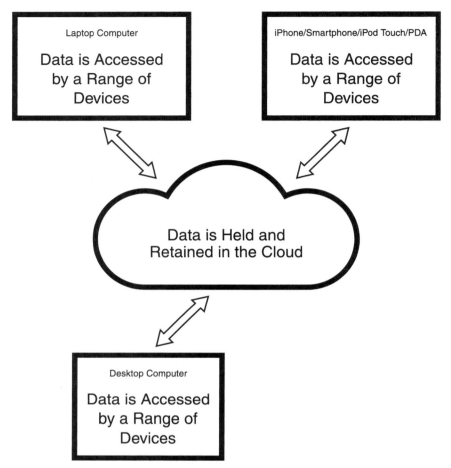

Figure 2.18   When data is stored in the cloud, you can access a single source of data and be certain that you have the most up-to-date information.

Now clearly, when you compare synchronization with the single data source approach, you will see that the single data source is a much more desirable approach. If you've ever tried using synchronization in practice (for instance, with a PDA), you will know that there can be some snags with synchronization, and often files cannot be readily compared, which leads to duplication or triplication of the data.

However, synchronization is crucial if you want to work offline. There will be times when you cannot access the internet—your connection may be down, you may be in the middle of nowhere with no net and no phone connection, or you may be locked in

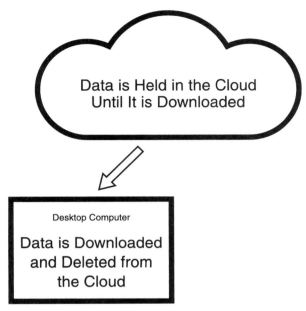

Figure 2.19 Data retrieval drags your information from the cloud and puts it onto your desktop computer.

a steel cage…. Whatever the reason, you can still work, and your computer/laptop/PDA/ cell phone will synchronize with the cloud when you are next able to make a connection.

Different tools allow you to synchronize in different ways. Some are more intelligent/ intuitive than others. The main options are:

- Automatic, where the local machine will check with the cloud at frequent intervals. While useful, this can add overhead to your computer's processing power.

- Manual, where you click a button to synchronize.

- Smart, which means when the tool is first opened, it makes a check and then it will only synchronize again when a file is changed.

And some do a combination of all of these things….

Email and the Cloud

Once you start to think about cloud services, you will probably consider the place where most people start with the cloud: email.

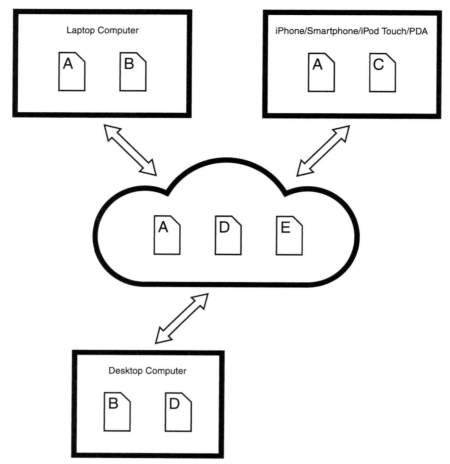

Figure 2.20   Data synchronization—the challenge is to make sure that the newer file overwrites the older file. There is often confusion about which file should be deleted and which should be kept!

You will usually access your email in one of two ways:

- Online through a web browser—for instance, if you are using Google Mail, then you are likely to access it through the web.

- Through an email client, such as Outlook Express or Outlook. By the way, you can access Google Mail with an email client such as Outlook.

Both of these options work, but there are downsides. Of course, there is a third way that addresses this issue.

At this point you may be thinking, "My internet service provider gives me email, and I can access that from the web... what am I doing here?" That's a valid point to a certain extent, however:

■   Your ISP's business is internet connection, not email. The focus of the company will be on the internet connection, with email being an add-on to lure you in. This may mean that the company is less concerned about making sure your email is as good as it can be (in terms of how well it runs, how quickly you can access and send emails, how much email you can send and receive, and how well/quickly it responds to problems such as spam).

■   If you ever want to leave your ISP—perhaps you can get a better deal, perhaps they have become too flaky—you will leave your email behind.

Neither of these issues may pose a problem from your perspective, but do give it some thought before you go with the default option.

Web Mail

Most of us are familiar with webmail, where you access your email through a browser, such as Chrome, Firefox, or Internet Explorer.

With webmail, all of your emails (both incoming and outgoing) are stored in the cloud. This is good (someone else looks after your data) and bad (someone else looks after your data *and* you need an internet connection to access it).

Webmail can also be a bit clunky to use, and the interface is often not as clean and slick as you might hope. Also, some webmail providers (particularly Google; see Figure 2.21) support their service with advertising, so whenever you check your mail, you will be facing advertising.

POP Mail

POP (or Post Office Protocol) email addresses many of the challenges of webmail. You install some software (such as Microsoft Outlook or Outlook Express), and that software manages your email.

The software works by retrieving your email and storing it in a local database in which a copy of your outgoing email correspondence is also stored. This will ensure that your email is kept in one place and you can find your correspondence even when your internet connection goes down. It also gives you much more speed: You don't have to wait for each email to open up when you have a slow internet connection.

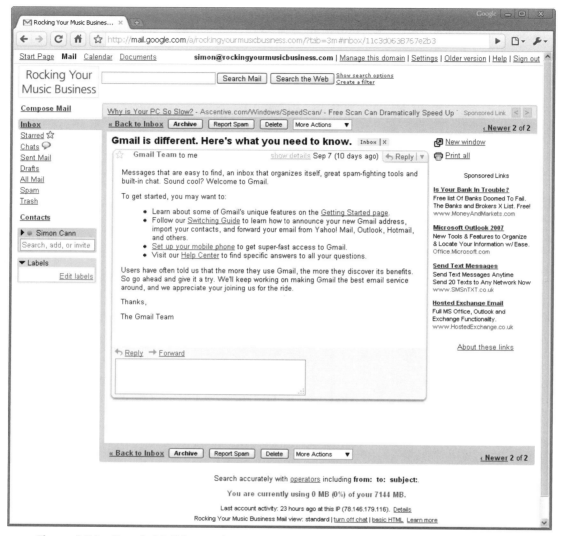

Figure 2.21 Google Mail is not the prettiest email service you will use, and as you can see on the right-hand side, there are advertisements that support the service.

The strength of this arrangement is also its challenge: Having a single source of data on a local machine means that your email records are vulnerable to hard disk failure (so you need to regularly back up your email database), and your correspondence is then not available when you're away from home (unless your email is on a laptop, which then makes your email vulnerable to loss/theft and so on).

IMAP Mail

Well surely there must be some way to combine the benefits of both systems, right?

There is: IMAP, or *Internet Message Access Protocol*. Think of this as being like having a specialized browser to access your webmail, and you will be getting close. With IMAP you have a specialized tool (an email client) to manage your email, which also gives you offline access to your email. With IMAP you can access your email wherever you are, so if you send an email when you're on the road, then you will have a copy of that email available on your desktop computer when you get home.

Many pieces of email software (such as Outlook and Thunderbird; see Figure 2.22) will give you both POP and IMAP access. However, some of these tools have little quirks—for

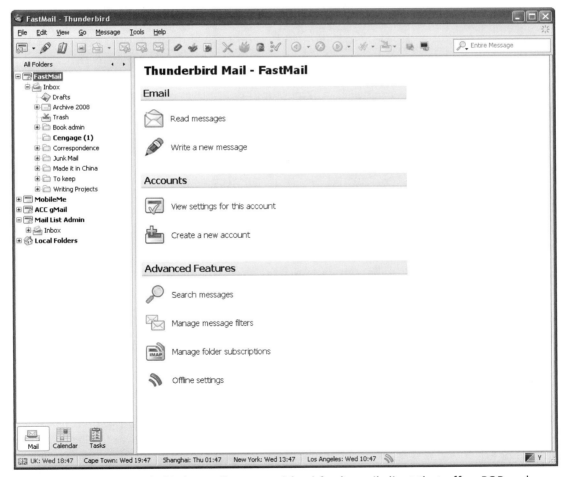

Figure 2.22 Thunderbird: a well-respected (and free) email client that offers POP and IMAP access. It is also the choice of this author.

instance, they will store outgoing emails locally and not on the cloud. Thunderbird is one of the email clients that avoids this problem, allowing you to keep your email in the cloud.

In order to use IMAP, your email provider must offer this service: Many, but not all, do. Equally, not all providers offer POP access, either. The ones least likely to offer either POP or IMAP are the free services supported by ads that need to encourage you to click. However, Google does offer both POP and IMAP with its free service.

Calendars and the Cloud

The facility to share calendars is a hugely powerful option, and there's a lot you can do with calendars.

The first thing to point out is that you don't need to only have one calendar—you can have many. As one example, Google—see Figure 2.23—allows you to set up as many calendars as you want. For instance, if you are a musician, you may want to have a work calendar and a home calendar. That way, you can make the work calendar available to your collaborators but keep any personal details in your home calendar (such as doctor visits) private.

Equally, if you are a band, you might have a working calendar to keep track of your appointments and a published calendar to tell your fans what you are up to. The published calendar can then be focused on your public appearances, so it might include gigs and TV/radio appearances or mention magazines where you are interviewed—if you have advance notice, you can include a note about the interview on the date that the magazine is published.

As I noted earlier, with the Google Calendar you can include location information, and a link to Google Maps will be included with your calendar feed (see Figure 2.24). This is clearly a hugely beneficial tool for helping your fans find a venue.
There are two sides to sharing:

- Making your calendar available, and

- Granting editing access rights.

Hopefully it goes without saying that you need some sort of a cloud provider to make your calendar available. If the calendar is stored on your local machine, then it will not be accessible. However, you do not necessarily need to use a cloud provider (although the Google Calendar is blissfully simple to use and share).

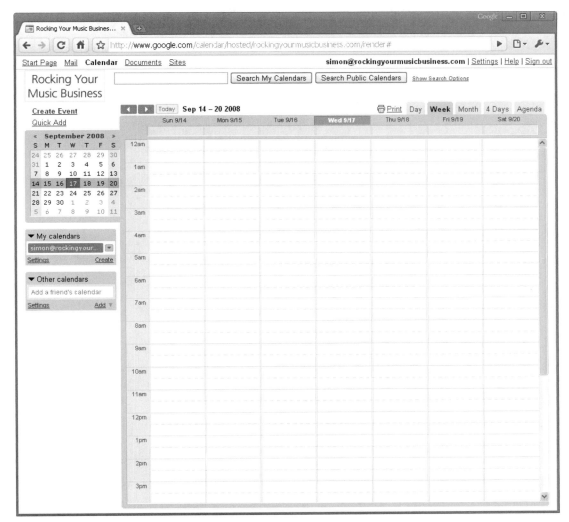

Figure 2.23   Google Calendar (note only one calendar has been set up here).

Publishing Your Calendar

One alternative is to publish your calendar to a WebDAV or CalDAV server. (I'll leave you to Google/Wikipedia these terms if you need.) If you are looking for a free provider that offers this service, then check out iCal Exchange (icalx.com), which hosts something like 100,000 calendars.

Generally, publishing a calendar is a fairly simple task. For instance, if you're looking for some free tools, then using the Lightning add-on in Thunderbird (mozilla.org/

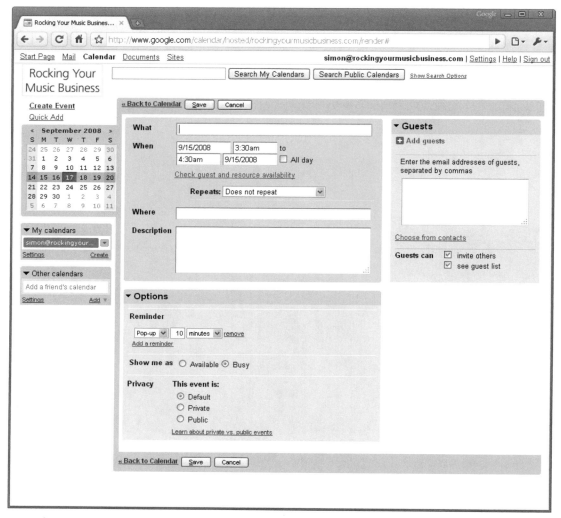

Figure 2.24 Creating an event in Google Calendar. There is the facility to include many details, including the location (in the Where box), which then links directly to Google Maps.

projects/calendar/lightning) or Sunbird (mozilla.org/projects/calendar/sunbird), you would select Calendar > Publish. You would then:

■ Choose the appropriate calendar to publish, and

■ Enter the location it is being published to—if you go with iCal Exchange, they will tell you what this is.

The publishing process takes seconds. You can then tell people where your calendar is located. This location will usually look like a long URL, but the file name will end with .ics, which is a standard calendar data format.

However, once you have published a calendar in this way, it is fixed and won't be updated if you change your local calendar. To update your calendar, you would need to re-publish, making sure that you keep the same file name (otherwise, people will still view the old calendar). As you can see, this can be a bit of a hassle, which is one of the reasons to use a shareable calendar.

Making Your Calendar Shareable

If you want to share your calendar, then the mechanics will be determined by your calendar's host (see Figure 2.25). Usually there are four options (with a few variations):

- Keep the calendar private.

- Share the calendar with everyone.

- Share the calendar with certain people.

- Show only free and busy time (so the details in your calendar will not be displayed).

With the sharing options, you also have the opportunity to give the person with whom you are sharing the calendar write access. This allows the person to add events and change items. Clearly, you need to be cautious about who can write to your calendar. For calendars that are going to be made available to the public, it is usually best to limit write access to a small number of people.

The great thing about having a shareable calendar is that your host will tell you the address of the feed that you need to tell people. Figure 2.26 shows the Google page explaining how I can share my calendar.

Subscribing to Calendar Feeds

The facility to subscribe to calendars can be incredibly useful—and you can use it to help your music business.

Say you want to add U.K. public holidays and Jewish festivals to your calendar. One option would be to look up these dates for yourself. However, there is a better option: Subscribe to calendar feeds. There are feeds covering almost every date-related subject, from holidays and festivals to the number of days the current U.S. President has in office and the weather. Many sports clubs also use this feature to publicize their fixtures, as do a number of leading bands.

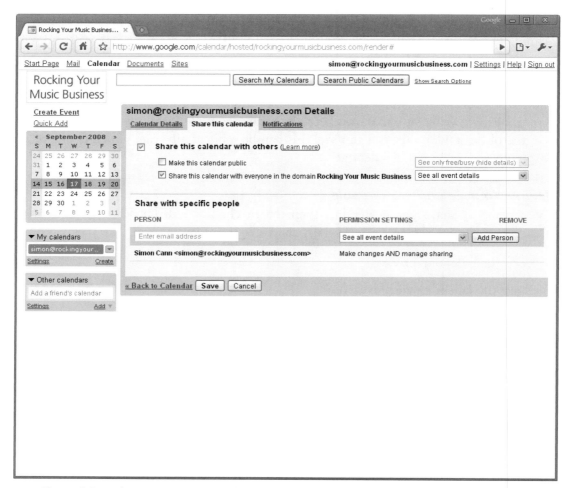

Figure 2.25 The access control options in the Google Calendar.

So once you start subscribing to a number of feeds, your calendar will no longer be "your" calendar, but rather a collection of calendars all brought together and displayed in one place. It sounds a bit confusing, but when you see it in practice, it is logical and compelling. When you start subscribing, you may also find you have a desire to subscribe to as many calendars as possible—you can do this, but then it becomes difficult to see which events matter and which are just interesting to know.

Your calendar software will allow you to subscribe to calendars in different ways.

- In Lightning/Sunbird, you can add a new calendar by selecting File > New > Calendar > On the Network, and then choosing the type of calendar feed and inputting the calendar's location.

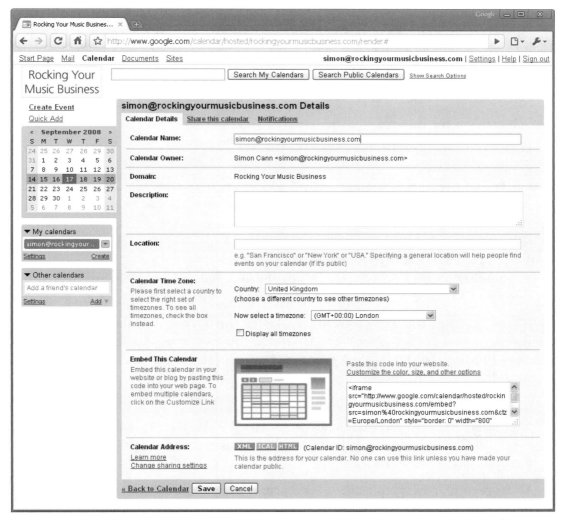

Figure 2.26 Sharing my Google Calendar. The important links are at the bottom of the page in the Calendar Address section.

■ In Google Calendar, under Other Calendars, select Add and then choose the type of calendar and its location.

For calendars that have limited access privileges, you may need to insert a password—the person who grants you access should tell you the password (unless they're just pretending to give you access!).

If you subscribe to a calendar that gives you write access, then once you have subscribed to the feed, you will also have the ability to edit and add to the calendar. Earlier I mentioned publishing a calendar, and then re-publishing as you update the calendar. This can be a hassle, so what you can do instead is:

- Publish the calendar.

- Subscribe to the calendar (having ensured you have write access).

- Delete the original calendar.

In this way you will be accessing (to read and write) the calendar that you have made public. This is a workaround; you will find it much easier to use Google!

VoIP: Cloud Computing for Phones?

VoIP is another of those nasty acronyms designed to hide a good idea. So what is VoIP and why do you care?

VoIP, or voice over internet protocol, is a system for making telephone calls over the internet. In a world of cell phones and landlines, you may be wondering why you would need this third option. While VoIP is not for everyone, there are some significant advantages to this approach:

- Cost. VoIP-to-VoIP calls are usually free (subject to the provider you use), even over long distances, even internationally. I am based in London and regularly talk to people in China, Africa, and the USA—these calls are all free (although clearly, I do pay for my internet connection).

- Multi-person. You can include several people on a single call—the only limit on the number of people is your computer's processing power.

- Accessibility is not limited to geography. As long as you can connect to the internet, you can make and receive calls. This means that as you move around, people only need to call one number to get hold of you, and this number will be the same irrespective of which country you are in.

- Quality. VoIP calls can be of a higher quality than conventional landline calls. I regularly talk with someone in L.A. (about 6,000 miles away). The VoIP call quality far exceeds the landline quality. However, because calls are routed over the internet, there can, of course, be challenges, especially if I am calling someone who has a poor internet connection at his or her end.

- This is the way the world is going. We're a long way from getting there, but in due course, all calls will be VoIP calls.

The current leader in the global VoIP market is Skype (skype.com), which is owned by PayPal. Skype offers many advantages:

- You can call out from their system to the conventional networks (landlines and cell phones); however, this does have a small cost, typically a cent per minute.

- You can have a conventional phone number (for a modest cost) so that people can call you from outside the system. You can also have different geographic numbers so that people can call you using local rates.

- You don't need to be connected to your computer—you can use a specialized WiFi handset to make calls.

There are other options. Vonage (vonage.com) offers a service, but at the moment their main focus is on replacing conventional phones in the home and office. Google also offer a service (Google Talk), but this is restricted to Google users.

Who Offers These Sorts of Cloud Services?

There are many firms offering cloud services in many different sorts of ways. However, the big players—including Amazon, Google, Microsoft, and Apple—understand that this is the next big thing and are making the cloud central to their business plans. Increasingly, these companies will be a significant part of how we all live our online lives in the next years. However, there are other players, so let's have a quick look at the various offerings.

I must point out that this book is being written in September 2008, so by the time you read it things may have changed significantly. In addition, my intention is not to advertise or recommend any of these services or to detail their full offerings—I am simply trying to give you an idea about what these services can do for you. You are going to have to do some research for yourself before you make any decisions about what is right for you.

Google

Google (google.com) is (currently) best-known for their search engine; however, in reality their whole business is about the cloud, which may be one of the reasons why they launched their own browser, Chrome (google.com/chrome). At the time of writing, Google offers perhaps the most comprehensive cloud offering (although I'm sure some of their competitors featured here would disagree).

Google's wide range of cloud-based services includes:

- Google Mail, an email service that also includes a contacts book (which can be shared if, and to the extent that, you want). You can access Google Mail through a web browser, through POP, and through IMAP.

- Google Calendar, a calendar service that lets you set up and share multiple calendars as well as view other people's calendars.

- Google Documents, a word processor, spreadsheet, and presentation package (all of which have features that are more than adequate for day-to-day use).

- Picasa, a photo sharing service, and YouTube, a video sharing service. With these services you can also embed photos and videos into your website.

- Maps—now, a map may seem like a map to you, but Google allows you to create customized maps (for instance, by marking locations) and also allows you to link maps to other tools. For instance, you can link a map to a calendar entry so not only can you tell people when you're playing, but you'll be able to give them a map to get there!

In addition, there is the Chrome browser, which, among other things, is designed to make working with the cloud easier. One example of this is that Google Gears (gears.google.com) is built into Chrome. Gears is the technology that allows Google cloud-based services to operate when you are offline.

One clear advantage that Google has is its pricing: It offers all these services for free—like many of Google's services, they are supported by advertising. Google does offer a "business" version that includes some additional features (such as additional storage space for emails), and this option allows you to switch the ads off.

Microsoft

Microsoft (microsoft.com) offers a range of services. Clearly, they have been offering Hotmail (perhaps the original web-based email service) for years. More recently, they have been making two significant moves into cloud computing:

- First, much of their existing range of Office tools has been given a web-based equivalent.

- Second, they are looking at a new service offering (called Mesh) that is intended to bring the whole cloud/tools/synchronization together.

Zoho

Perhaps the most directly comparable competitor to the Google office tools suite is Zoho (zoho.com). In many ways, Zoho takes the notion of an office in the cloud and out-Googles Google—certainly, there are a lot more tools in this suite than there are in the Google office suite, as Figure 2.27 indicates. This is some of what Zoho offers (at the moment—there's sure to be more by the time this book is published):

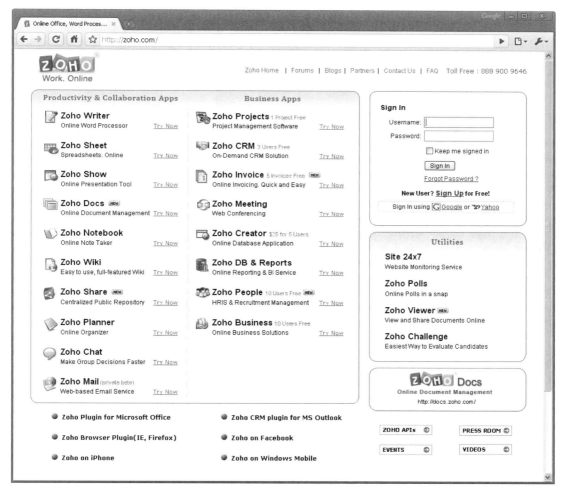

Figure 2.27   The Zoho website.

- Zoho Writer, a word processor.
- Zoho Sheet, a spreadsheet.

- Zoho Show, a presentation tool.

- Zoho Notebook, a notetaker.

- Zoho Wiki, a wiki creator/manager.

- Zoho Share, a centralized repository. Zoho files can be individually shared by Zoho (and if you create a business account, that sharing can be limited within the business). Zoho Share allows all types of documents to be shared (for instance, Word documents) and for the sharing (whether of Zoho files or other file types) to be to anyone anywhere on the internet.

- Zoho Chat, a tool to facilitate communication in a number of ways, including chat and instant messenger tools.

- Zoho Mail, a web-based email service. At the moment Zoho Mail doesn't offer POP or IMAP access.

- Zoho Invoice, a tool to create and issue invoices.

- Zoho Creator, a database tool.

As noted, this is just a summary of what Zoho offers, and these tools are all free. Zoho offers other free tools and has a range of additional paid-for services. (For instance, you pay if you want more storage space than the basic allowance or when you get past issuing a certain number of invoices.) However, the paid-for services are a very good value.

You may have noticed that there is a gap in Zoho's offerings: There is no calendaring facility yet.

Apple

Apple offers MobileMe (me.com; see Figure 2.28), which is yours for an annual subscription of $99. It is primarily aimed at helping people keep their various bits of hardware linked together. At the moment, some of the sharing isn't quite as powerful as that offered by, say, Google, although I'm sure it will get there. However, if you have an iPhone or an iPod Touch, then MobileMe can do good things for you.

MobileMe includes:

- Email, which is accessible as a webmail service or through POP or IMAP (and, of course, it's a breeze to set up with your iPhone/iPod Touch).

- Calendar (while these can be accessible on all of your own devices, currently they cannot be shared with other people).

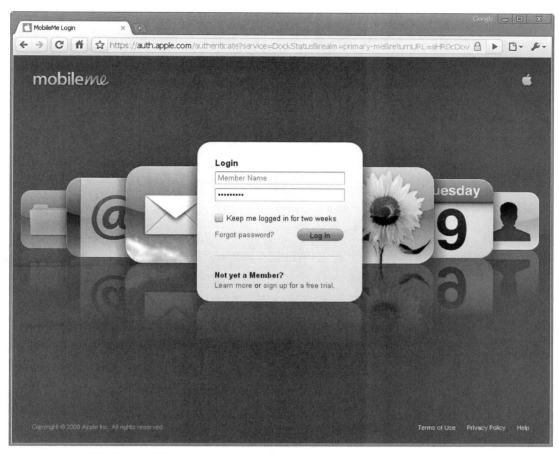

Figure 2.28   The MobileMe login screen for online access.

- Contacts management. You can store a huge amount of data about your contacts, and your contacts can be synchronized between your desktop computer and your iPhone while being web-accessible, but you can't share your contacts with other people.

- Photo gallery. Unlike your calendar and contacts, photos can be shared.

- File storage. MobileMe allows huge quantities of file storage and has the facility to then share files (but with security, so you don't need to make your private documents publicly available).

Although it's just a music store at the moment, I wouldn't be surprised if one day iTunes morphs into some sort of cloud service too (but for music, obviously!). However, this is just my hunch, and it's not here today (so don't go looking for it—and don't write to me if it never happens). Also, before it becomes a cloud service, Apple is (not unreasonably) going to need to figure a way to make money out of it.

Amazon

Amazon has approached cloud computing from a different direction. Instead of chasing the consumer market, it is bringing its expertise to bear by creating one of the most powerful behind-the-scenes infrastructure operations. This infrastructure is then being made available for developers to create consumer/end-user services.

Amazon Web Services (AWS; aws.amazon.com), as it is called, offers several pieces to their service:

- Amazon Simple Storage Service (Amazon S3) is a storage service where digital files can be stored.

- Amazon Elastic Compute Cloud (Amazon EC2) is a web service that offers scalable processing. This is most suitable for developers looking to build an interactive service.

The service that really interests us is S3 (the Simple Storage Service), which allows files to be stored in a secure form so that only you can access them. Indeed, you can even encrypt the files so that Amazon could never read them. Alternatively, your files could be made accessible (either for a regular download or as a source for a BitTorrent-type distribution).

You can't just sign up with Amazon and get your storage space. Instead, you need to acquire some other software that will act as the conduit between you and Amazon S3. Once you have paid for that, you will then need to pay for Amazon storage space. This may seem odd—and to an extent it is—but it does have benefits.

They key benefit is that you are only paying for storage space that you use, and the scale of charges is published. So if you store 1 GB of files, then all you will pay is 15 cents for each month of storage. If you have more files, then you pay more, and if you have no files stored, then you will pay nothing. You only pay for what you use, which means that your costs are highly controllable (although you may find they are sufficiently low that you don't need to worry too hard about controlling them).

There is also a data transfer charge. Again, this is likely to be comparatively modest if you are using the service to back up your files. However, it may be more significant if you are using it as a source from which files may be downloaded. If you are using the service in this way, you may want to consider setting up a BitTorrent-style download.

BitTorrent is a peer-to-peer file sharing protocol that can be used to distribute large amounts of data—for instance, you may want to make a track or a whole CD available for download. The initial distributor of the file acts as the first "seed." Each peer who downloads the data from the seed then distributes the files to other peers. When someone then downloads a file, they do not download it from the seed, but from a number of peers. This reduces the load on the seed and also provides excess capacity within the system, making the download more robust.

Although this may seem like a lot of trouble, it is much easier in practice than this explanation may suggest. The key reason why you may want to create a torrent rather than a simple download is to take the load off your website. A conventional download can overload and crash your website. A torrent is far less likely to do this.

As I said, you need separate software to access Amazon S3. Here are two examples:

- Jungle Disk (jungledisk.com) is primarily a backup utility that you can use to back up all or specified files at regular intervals. However, it can have a wider use in allowing you to share files within a limited and secure group of individuals. As with many S3-related tools, this group of people can grow and contract at will, meaning that there is no infrastructure decision to including people within the group. Another key advantage of Jungle Disk is that it will run on Windows, Mac, and Linux machines.

- Bucket Explorer (bucket explorer.com) is like Windows Explorer (or any other file manager) but for Amazon S3. However, it lets you do more than simply upload and download files to and from S3 and browse files. For instance, you can:
  - Load HTML files so you can use your S3 space as a basic website (which you may want to do if there will be a lot of downloads and no user interactions).
  - Set server access logging (which sounds dull, but can be useful for audit purposes).
  - Synchronize data between computers.
  - Create public URLs and time-limited signed URLs to share your files stored on Amazon S3—you can also create torrent "seeds."
  - Access other people's files on S3.
  - Set access and security permissions on each and every file to prevent unauthorized access.

While there is some overlap between Jungle Disk and Bucket Explorer, the two tools essentially achieve separate tasks. However, they are both dependent upon S3.

Adobe

Adobe is getting into the game with its Acrobat (acrobat.com; see Figure 2.29), which is probably intentionally confused with Adobe Acrobat, its PDF creator/editor/viewer. Acrobat contains a limited number of tools, but these are intended to help with document sharing and collaboration. The suite includes:

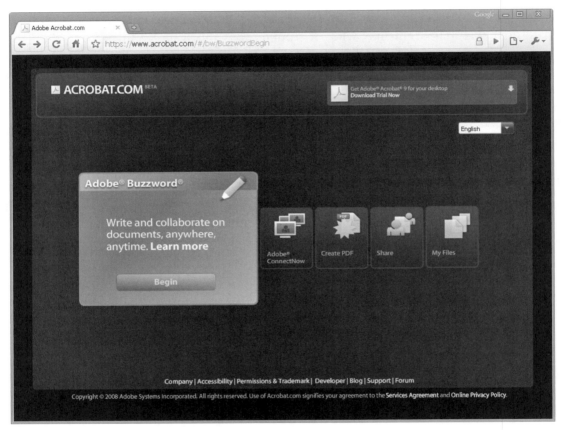

Figure 2.29   The acrobat.com website.

- Buzzword, a document creator and editor.

- ConnectNow, a tool to facilitate online meetings and desktop sharing (so you can literally show someone what's on your computer screen).

- PDF Create, a tool to create PDFs (although this appears to only allow five PDFs to be created, after which you have to pay to use this part of the service).

- Share, a tool specifically designed to manage your sharing (so you can grant and revoke privileges).

- My Files, an online file storage space for documents created within Acrobat as well as other documents you might want to store and share.

Acrobat is interesting and is a free service in its basic form, but it lacks many features that may be useful for a musician running his or her business. For instance, there is no spreadsheet tool and there is no calendar. Oh yeah... there's no email.

And More...

This list of examples doesn't begin to cover the market for cloud services, which are available in many different forms. Here are a few more examples:

- Virtually every email provider offers some sort of cloud services. Usually this is just web-enabled email, but often other services are offered that make the service more cloud-friendly (such as IMAP access). Some also offer extras such as address book synchronization and web storage space.

- Mozilla is currently trialing a service called Weave (labs.mozilla.com/projects/weave), which will run within its Firefox browser. The idea behind Weave is to make the web "mobile" so that however and wherever you access the web, you will have the same data. Weave will achieve this goal by storing in the cloud your bookmarks (favorites), your browsing history, and your passwords, so you can access these whenever and however you access the web. There are other tools to duplicate bookmarks and the like, but this is quite an ambitious project.

I highlighted two of the cloud office suite providers: Google and Zoho. There are, of course, other providers who are very serious about their business but may not have the traction of the bigger services. These include:

- ContactOffice (contactoffice.com), which offers a good range of office tools, including mail, word processing, spreadsheets, task lists, bookmark sharing, and so on.

- Zimbra (zimbra.com), which is a Yahoo! company. Zimbra tools are focused on messaging and collaborating. Unlike the others, the tools are not accessible directly at Zimbra's website. Instead, Zimbra makes its software freely available for other providers to implement (often at a cost, as the provider will be providing the servers and the support).

Hardware Costs

While many of the cloud services are free or incredibly cheap, there are still costs associated with putting your business into the cloud. One is the cost of transition—which is mentioned in the upcoming "Making the Choice between the Cloud and the Desktop" section)—and the other is the cost of hardware. Here there is good news.

If you put all of your computing into the cloud, then your future costs should fall. For instance, there will be no need for:

- Servers (mail servers and file storage servers)—everyone associated with your business will just need an internet connection. Because everyone will be connected to the internet, no additional infrastructure will be necessary. As well as saving on hardware costs, this will save on support engineers, too.

- Powerful computers to run the latest software. Your computers should last much longer, and you will be able to use cheaper or free software (such as Linux), which will give you another savings.

The main cost—unless you are going to run your business from an internet café—is a computer with an internet connection. However, you may have more devices—for instance, a desktop for your home base and an iPod/cell phone when you're on the road. Perhaps you might also have an ultra portable or a laptop, too. But if you already own this stuff, then there won't be an extra cost.

Why Hasn't Everyone Else Done This Already?

Clearly, there are disadvantages to this cloud approach. As I've already mentioned, you will be reliant on your internet connection. However, in case of the infrequent occurrence of this going down, you can store data locally and upload any new data once the connection is restored. Equally, in a wired-up world, you're probably already quite reliant on your internet connection.

The other obvious downside is that the online tools (such as the word processor and spreadsheets) generally have fewer features than their Microsoft (and other name-brand) equivalents. However, they always have the important features, and the tools that are missing are usually the more specialized ones. Indeed, some may see this simplicity as an advantage: It makes them easier to learn and easier to use, and there are fewer distractions.

There is a clear trend for the wider acceptance of cloud computing—the likes of Microsoft, Apple, and Adobe would not be doing what they are doing if they didn't think that cloud computing will be highly significant. As the reliability and practicability of the tools are proven and the features are expanded, cloud computing will see wider adoption.

At the moment, there are many providers trying to get into the market. As with anything new, a lot of these companies will promise the earth and will then suddenly disappear without a trace. One thing that may change is the pricing.

My hunch is there will still be free providers—as an example, I would still expect Google to be around in five years with its free advertising-supported services. However, I would not see it as being unreasonable for there to be costs—annual service costs—which would be much less than the equivalent of desktop software. Where there are costs—in particular for storage and data transfer—these are likely to fall over the longer term as the underlying hardware gets cheaper and consumers benefit from efficiencies of scale.

So why haven't people changed yet? Well, I would suggest a combination of:

- Inertia—it's always easiest to stick with what you've got.

- Fear of the unknown.

- Ignorance—these tools are still new and developing. Once you try using them—particularly when you try the tools in combination and start sharing with your friends and work colleagues—you will see a whole new world of possibility and ease of workflow open up.

Desktop Computing

So if that's cloud computing, what's the alternative?

The alternative is what we've had for very many years: desktop computing. With desktop computing, you have a standalone machine (which may be a desktop computer, a laptop, or an ultra portable) on which all your software is loaded and all your files are stored. These computers will usually be attached to the internet (for email and web browsing) and may also be attached to a network for file and/or printer sharing.

Just to ensure there is no confusion, you can't go to a computer store and buy a desktop computer or a cloud computer. You buy a computer—how you use it determines whether you are doing the desktop thing or the cloud thing.

Equally, please realize that you can never completely get away from the cloud or the desktop. For instance, if you want to use email, then you are going to have to interact with the cloud. Equally, in order to function, every computer needs its own operating system (and if it is going to access the cloud, at the very minimum it will usually need a browser such as Chrome, Firefox, or Internet Explorer). In short, it's not an either/or choice: It's all a question of degrees.

What's Good about Desktop Computing?

There are many advantages to desktop computing:

- The prime advantage to desktop is that it is very familiar to everyone who has used a computer. Most people will have used Word and other Microsoft tools at some point, and these tools usually fulfill their functions very well.

- Everything you need is there on the computer in front of you—you have your own little closed universe and know where it is.

- With desktop computing, you are not dependent on an internet connection (except when you need to interact with the outside world, for instance to send an email).

- There is a lot of really good software available, and this software has been tried and tested over many years and has been proved to work reliably. There's also a lot of really excellent free software available. If the free option appeals to you—and it should, because you want to spend your money on music, not software—then check out the Open Office software (openoffice.org). Although it has one or two rough edges, this will perform all of the main functions that can be accomplished by Microsoft Office.

What's Bad about Desktop Computing?

There are, of course, disadvantages to desktop computing:

- You are highly dependent on your hardware. If your hardware goes down for whatever reason, then you will lose access—maybe temporarily, perhaps permanently—to your data. Even if you have been rigorous with your backups, you are still likely to lose some information. Also, if you are dependent on a certain hardware/software combination to access your information, then you may not be able to immediately access your backup.

- The cost of software is comparatively high. Windows may be bundled with your machine, but a full suite of office software may have a comparatively high price tag attached to it.

- You need to make decisions, and these will have implications for years to come. Once you have made the decision to go with Windows as your operating system, then it may be quite a challenge to choose an office suite that isn't produced by Microsoft (however, taking Open Office as an example, there are options). Equally, if you go down the Apple route, then any software you purchase must be compatible with the Mac operating system. To change from Apple to Microsoft or vice versa could necessitate the purchase of a whole new suite of software in addition to the acquisition of a new computer.

- Your data will be accessible from only one machine—the machine on which it is stored. This will make sharing harder (although it does have beneficial implications for data security).

Making the Choice between the Cloud and the Desktop

So you've sat down and considered cloud computing and the desktop alternatives, and you're wondering which way to jump.

Can I make a suggestion? Don't decide one way or the other—do both.

These are not either/or decisions—you can do both, and you need to apply some common sense here. For instance, if you already have a desktop set up, then don't throw that away—instead, look at some of the sensible things you could do to enhance your setup. Equally, if you have yet to set up your office, then take a serious look at the cloud—many of the tools are free, which will help you keep a tight rein on your costs.

However, in the longer term, the cloud is where there will be a lot of focus, and it will increasingly be a *de facto* part of our online existence and how we all do business.

The cloud will mean that you can work independently of your location and your hardware—in other words, you will be able to work anywhere and with any tool. So if you're in Kuala Lumpur and your laptop has suddenly gone missing, with the cloud you could borrow a computer/PDA/ultra portable or go to an internet café and carry on working. If you're reliant on a specific machine—and that machine is not available for whatever reason—then your business stops. When your business stops, so does your income.

As well as being hardware and geography independent, the cloud means that you can also be operating system impartial. In other words, it won't matter whether you want to use Windows, Mac OS, Linux, or any new operating system—as long as you've got a browser, you'll be fine.

As I keep saying, this isn't an either/or choice; however, there are some things that you probably should put into the cloud now, even if you want to carry on with a desktop setup. These include:

- Email. All sent and received email should be stored in the cloud so you can access your email from anywhere. Ideally, you should be able to access your email by a web browser and through IMAP (so that sent emails will be stored on the cloud too).

- If your email is in the cloud, then so should your contacts be. There's nothing worse than getting lost on the way to a gig and knowing that the promoter's name and phone number are back at home and that you didn't put the details on your phone. If these details are on the cloud, then you could use your cell phone to browse the net and pick up the details. Better still, you could automatically synchronize your contacts held on the cloud to your cell phone (and so the promoter's name and contact number would already be there for you). A service such as NuevaSync (nuevasync.com) could be just what you need for this sort of synchronization.

- Calendars—in my opinion—need to be in the cloud if they are going to be shared.

- Files. You may not want to immediately move all of your files into the cloud, but you should probably start backing up to the cloud (for instance, by using Jungle Disk or similar software). This will give you data security and it will also mean that you can access your files in the cloud. Although it may not offer an immediate "single source of data" solution, this would give you greater protection than simply relying on a hard drive. That being said, Jungle Disk allows you to set up a virtual network drive (in other words, the equivalent of a hard drive, but in the cloud), which can then be shared. This would allow you to have cloud storage of your data. Jungle Disk also allows you to access your data through a web browser, so you have flexibility.

In all things, remember that this is not a question about whether Mac or PC is best (or whether Linux beats both of them). This is not an attempt to break the dominance of Microsoft or to make sure you won't be paying "the man." This is pure pragmatism. You need to do what is best for you and find a solution that works for you and that is both (1) secure and (2) practical.

File Format

So are we there now? Have we made all the decisions we need to make? Nearly, but not quite.

There's still one further factor to think about: file formats. Let me be honest: This is tedious. However, it is important, so you do need to think about it.

File format is important for a number of reasons:

- First, if you are going to be sharing information with other people, then you need to be able to share it in a form that they can read. You may have the whizziest word processor in the whole country, but if you're the only person who can open files with that format, then it doesn't count for much.

- Second, longevity. Stuff changes over time. What worked once won't work at a later date. File formats are no different, and over time they change. This means that current file formats may fall into disuse at a later date, making those files inaccessible. Let me give you a parallel: Twenty years ago we stored data on 5.25-inch floppy disks. Have you seen a slot for one of those recently? Okay, you can find places that can still read these disks, but you need to try hard (and you will probably have to pay money). Now think how hard it is to read file formats from 20 years ago.

Assuming I've convinced you (or beaten you into submission), then what should you be using and what should you be avoiding?

Which File Formats Should I Use?

There is a whole range of document formats, and it can be quite confusing trying to choose the right one.

Word/Excel Formats

At the time of writing, Microsoft Word and Excel (and PowerPoint) have the most widely read formats. Most people will be able to open documents in those formats, even if they are not using those tools.

So if you're looking for the most shareable format at the moment, this is it. Added to which, due to its all-pervading prevalence, I would guess that many systems will continue to be able to read these formats for a good while yet, so you'll still be able to access your Word and Excel documents in 10 years (but don't shout at me if you can't and you didn't look after your documents).

Naturally, Word and Excel can open and save documents in their own formats. In addition, you can open and save documents in these formats with the Open Office suite, Google Docs, and Zoho Writer, among others.

PDF: Portable Document Format

The PDF format is also currently very popular.

While it is possible to edit PDFs with specialized tools, PDFs are generally intended to share read-only documents, so the format may not be appropriate when more than one person is collaborating on a document.

However, like Word and Excel formats, due to the current prevalence of the file type, documents stored in this format are likely to remain readable for many years.

Text and HTML

If you're looking for the most widely readable document format and the format that is likely to have the greatest longevity, there is only one answer: the text (.txt) format. This literally stores the text of a document and nothing else—so there is no formatting or any of the other niceties (such as bold, underlining, or different fonts) to aid the presentation of the document.

However, everyone (who can open electronic documents) can read the format, and this is likely to remain the case indefinitely (unless someone invents a new alphabet).

HTML (or *Hypertext Markup Language*) is another text format. As its name suggests, it also includes code within the text to indicate formatting and to add hypertext links. For instance, there will be codes to say "start bold text here" and "end bold text here" or "link the following text to this destination on the internet."

HTML is primarily designed for text that will be viewed on the internet or through other electronic media. Like text, it has the benefit of longevity, but as it includes the marking up, it can be a bit cumbersome to read the raw text when it is not rendered through a browser. However, like text, any HTML document should be readable for many years to come.

Another significant advantage of text and HTML is that there are no embedded elements within the files, so viruses cannot be included within these files.

ODF: Open Document Format

The Open Document Format is growing in popularity. Documents in this format can be opened and saved in Google Docs, Zoho, Open Office, and the most recent versions of Microsoft Office products.

The aim behind the format—which covers spreadsheets, charts, presentations, and word processing documents—is to create a standard that many different software developers can adopt. This will ensure that documents can be swapped between different operating systems without errors.

The format stores the data as marked-up text (like HTML, but more complicated for detailed formatting), which is then compressed to minimize space. As a text-based format, these files should be accessible for a long time in the same manner that text and HTML files should be.

There is another format that is sometimes confused with ODF: Office Open XML (OOXML), which was originally developed by Microsoft. At the moment this particular format does not seem to have any use beyond Microsoft documents.

Cloud Formats

The cloud document services don't give you an option about the format in which you save documents in the cloud. However, they give you lots of export options so you can always put your document into another format that can be read by another program.

The main export options are Word, text, HTML, ODF, and PDF, which covers most, if not all, of the options you want.

Which File Formats Should I Avoid?

In short, avoid any format unless it is widely accepted in very many places and by very many pieces of software. Here are a few formats that you may want to avoid (and please note, this is not anywhere near a comprehensive list):

- WordPerfect format. About 15 years ago, WordPerfect was the dominant word processor and Word was sneered at—times have changed! Many pieces of software can read WordPerfect format, but often there will be formatting errors and unstable documents when these documents are opened in other systems. If you have any old WordPerfect documents, now is the time to convert them. (If you're unsure what to convert them to, then convert them to text, Word, and any other format you can think of.)

- Specialized Mac formats and specialized Linux formats. You may have the greatest piece of software, and it may create the most elegant file format from an engineering perspective. However, 99 percent of the population won't be able to open these documents today, so don't use the format.

- Any format with encryption. Encryption will stop you from being able to open documents in other formats, so don't do it.

- MultiMate, WordStar, or anything else from the 1980s. These packages might have been good once, but no one uses them anymore, so don't keep your files in that format.

The notion of file formats is not an argument about what is "best." What matters is making sure that your document will be available to the widest number of people in the fastest and easiest manner, and that you will still be able to open your archives in five, ten, fifteen, or more years.

So How Do I Get Set Up?

The time, money, and effort to get set up will depend on which course (or courses) you choose and what tools you have on hand already.

If you want to go with a conventional office and desktop machine and desktop software, then you will need:

- Somewhere to put all your equipment

- Furniture, such as chairs and desks

- A computer (or several) and all the things that go with a computer, such as printers and cables to join everything

- Software to run on the computer

- An internet connection (if you want to communicate with the outside world)

And that's pretty much it—go down to your local computer store, and you can be up and running as soon as you have unpacked the boxes and installed the software. If that's what you want, then you can skip the rest of this chapter.

However, you might also want to put some of your business into the cloud. You may even want your whole business in the cloud. If you're following this route, then you will need:

- Devices to access the cloud—these could include a computer (desktop, laptop, or ultra mobile), a PDA/phone that can access the internet (such as a Smartphone, an iPhone, or an iPod Touch), or a local internet café. Any hardware will, of course, need the appropriate software to access the internet—this is almost always included.

- A way to connect to the internet (if you don't already have it—this is more of an issue for computer users). However, you will also need to figure out how to access the internet when you're on the move—a phone with internet access (such as a Smartphone/iPhone) will be quite good, but there are many areas of little coverage. Take some time to think about what you will do in these regions.

- Your cloud services up and running.

- You may also want a printer if you want to produce hard copies (for instance, if you need to send a letter).

The remainder of this section looks at how to get your business set up in the cloud.

Making the Choice between Cloud Providers

So how do you make the choice if you need to set up your office today? Sure, there are many services out there, but which one is right for you?

There are several ways you can make this decision. Perhaps the simplest is to go with the current market leader in this area: Go with Google. In the current market, that would be a good choice. Equally, if I had to put a bet on which company will still be around and offering these services in five years, I would bet on Google.

However, that is not a particularly rigorous approach, particularly for a business book, so I do recommend you review your choices before you make a decision. In making your decision, you might want to think about the following:

- First, figure out what you need to run your business (and clearly you need to read the rest of this book to give you some help). If you can do everything with email, then don't look at word processors.

- Once you know what you need, rule out any provider who doesn't meet your needs. I don't think you need to stick with one provider; however, you may initially find it easier.

- Although one provider will be easier, don't rule out using different providers for different tasks. (For instance, use Google for their Docs and Zoho for their database functionality.)

- Figure out what you know. If there is a provider who you are familiar with and the price is good, then seriously think about going with them. Do you really want to re-learn how to use a set of business tools?

- Check out your potential providers. Many are free, and most give you a free test option, so you have nothing to lose apart from time and your temper. Give the systems a "real life" try and see which work the best.

- See how well data can be transferred in and out of the system (so if you make the wrong choice you can go elsewhere, and you aren't locked into one provider). Equally, check to see whether you are signing up for a minimum contract.

One issue you need to consider is the cost and mechanics of transition—the cost and process of getting from where you are to where you want to be. Here you have several options:

- The clean break. Ignore everything that has gone before and start with a clean sheet of paper. This is appealing, but you may find that you have old emails or letters to which you might want to refer.

- Transfer everything. Transfer all of your emails to the cloud, upload all of your documents to the cloud (changing their formats as they go), and so on. Depending on how much data you already have, this may be quite a challenge.

There is a third option: Use your common sense. Only transfer recent and relevant material, and only transfer archive material if it is easy—for instance, it will probably be harder to sort which emails are recent/relevant than to transfer all of your emails. By contrast, you might only want to transfer copies of any contracts to the cloud rather than all your documents.

Perhaps the biggest cost in making the transition will be your time investment—the time in making the transfers and the time in learning your new system. Although this may all seem like a chore and a big investment, you will save so much time and money over the years that it will pay dividends.

Setting Up the Cloud Office: How's It Done?

At its most basic, all you need to do to set up a cloud office is sign up for a service. This usually involves giving the service your name and email address—you then create a user name and password, and you're up and running. While most services are that simple, if you're running your business in the cloud, then you're likely to want to do more. For instance, you probably want to share your documents within a limited group of people. You might also want to do other things, such as have an email address for the band that reflects the band's web address.

Rather than discuss all the things you could do and go through all the permutations of the options, let me show you how you can set up a cloud office with Google. I'm using Google for this example because:

- You can attach your own URL (web address).

- The email system is good.

- The calendar system is good.

- The documents/spreadsheets/presentations are good.

- You can share a lot of things, and there are tools to help with this. (For instance, you can set up a website where access is limited to certain individuals, there is a chat facility, and there is a VoIP phone option.)

Please don't take this as a recommendation. I am simply using Google because it does all the basics and is free (so you can safely try this at home). If you want to test a cloud office, then it's an easy place to go and there is little risk. However, I do recommend you look at other options before making your decision and find what works best for your business.

There is also a paid version of the Google service (which I am not using for this illustration). The paid service offers some additional features:

- Secure private video sharing

- More email storage (more than three times the volume) and the option to exclude the ads that accompany your emails

- A virtual conference room facility

- More security features

- Phone support

Google also offer other paid services, such as email archiving and specialized email security. Unless you are getting very corporate, you probably won't be very interested in those offerings.

First Steps: Sign Up

To get set up with Google Apps for your business (rather than just setting up a Google email account), go to google.com/a and sign up. As you can see in Figure 2.30, if you already have a URL, you will be able to use that. Alternatively, you can purchase a new one as part of the signup process. If you want to know more about getting hold of your own domain and controlling your own domain, then check out Chapter 4, which gives further detail.

As part of the signup, you will be asked to enter a few details (such as your name) and to sign a user agreement. Once you have finished, you should reach a screen that looks something like Figure 2.31. You will notice that "Not active" is noted next to every tool, and there is a warning sign that to activate the services, the domain ownership must be verified.

Google gives you two options to verify your domain:

- Put an HTML page on your website that has a name specified by Google.

- Change one of the records in your DNS listing. The DNS (*Domain Name System*) listing is the listing with your domain registrar that tells the internet where your domain is located.

Uploading an HTML page is the easier option, but then again, as you will see in the next section, it is quite useful to be able to tweak the DNS records. Once you have completed

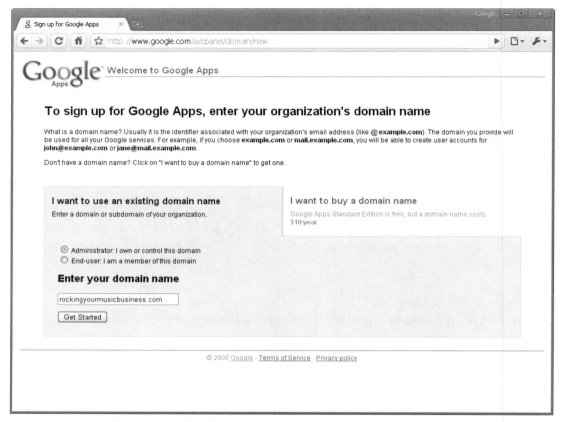

Figure 2.30 To get started with Google Apps, enter your domain and click Get Started.

the action to verify your account, it can take around 24 hours for Google to confirm that everything is in order.

Setting Up Easy URLs

Instead of going to my login page and then navigating to whichever tool I want to go to, it is possible to set up easy URLs. This means that I can go to mail.rockingyourmusicbusiness. com to get to my mail or calendar.rockingyourmusicbusiness.com to access my calendar.

The process to set this up is straightforward enough, but it does involve some copying and pasting.

To set up the URL, first select the tool to which you wish to assign the URL. As you can see in Figure 2.32, I have selected the Calendar.

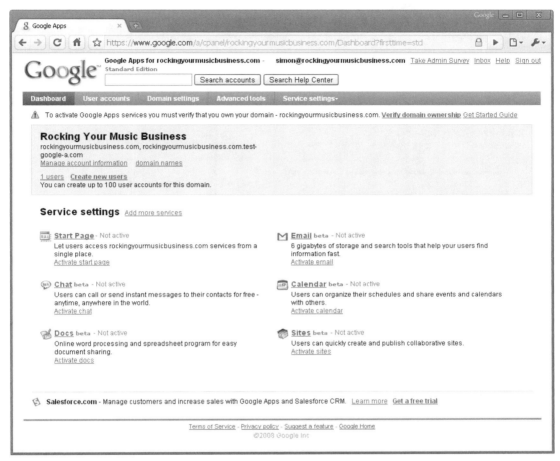

Figure 2.31 After signing up for Google Apps, you still have to do a bit of work to get everything sorted out. Notice, too, the warning to verify domain ownership.

As you can see, there are two choices:

- The default URL: google.com/calendar/a/rockingyourmusicbusiness.com.

- One you set yourself. As you can see, I have gone for one that is far more logical and memorable: calendar.rockingyourmusicbusiness.com

In this case, the sub-domain (in other words, the "calendar" bit in the domain) can be selected by you. You don't need to use the word calendar—I did because that's what it is and so, for my small brain, this makes life easier.

Having added the sub-domain, click on the Continue button, which leads you to a screen that looks like Figure 2.33. This tells you about changing your DNS records

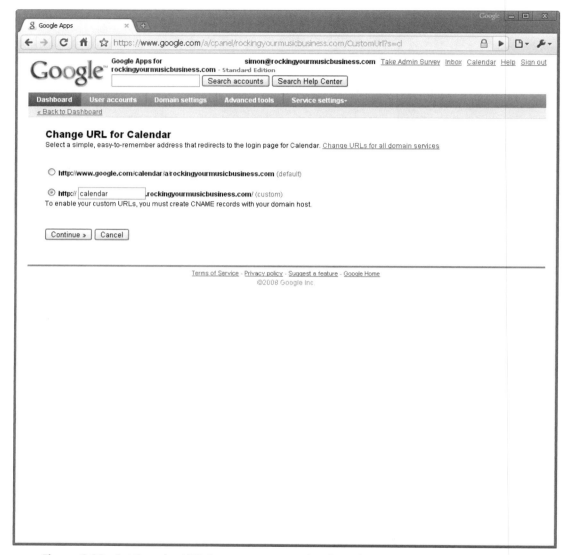

Figure 2.32 Setting the URL (or more accurately, the sub-domain) for the Calendar.

(so that not only can your main website be found, but your sub-domains—which will be in a different place, on Google servers—can be located, too).

This screen tells you everything you need to know; however, you still have to manually change the DNS records at your registrar, so it's not *that* simple. So what do you do? Well, log in to your registrar, open the DNS record, and add a line that looks like line six in Figure 2.34.

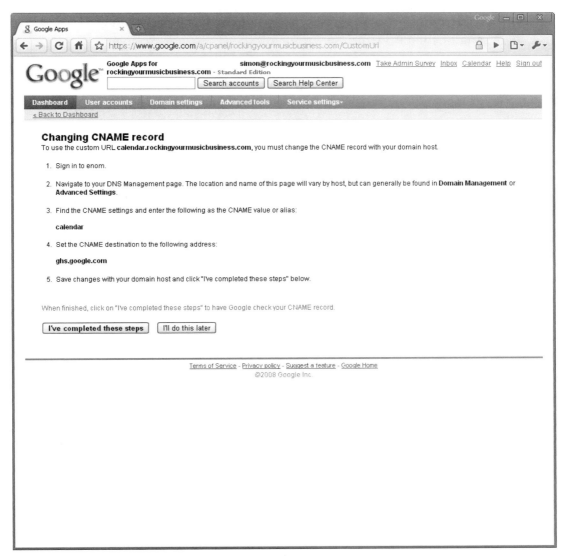

Figure 2.33   Instructions for changing the CNAME record when setting up an easy URL.

Once you have changed the DNS record and saved it, go back to Google and click on the I've Completed These Steps button. That's it—you're done. Your easy URL is now set up. You can go back and repeat the process for all of your main tools (which, as you can see from Figure 2.35, I have done).

Setting Up Email

It is slightly more complicated to set up email.

First off, you can set up the sub-domain, as noted a moment ago. This is the easy part. The tedious part is routing the email. In the same way that the DNS record for your website tells people where your web pages are stored on the internet, the DNS settings also tell any email messages that are addressed to you where your email mailbox lives. So if your email box for you@yourdomain.com is going to live on Google and be part of the Google Mail system, then you need to change your DNS records.

Thankfully, you don't need any technical knowledge, but you do need cutting and pasting skills to achieve this. Look back to Figure 2.34, and you will see the appropriate settings *for my domain* in lines 12 to 18. Google will automatically display the settings you need to punch in, and all you have to do is copy the settings to the DNS record that is held by your registrar.

Once you have created those records, all emails addressed to your domain will be sent to your Google account. Clearly some mail you will want, but you may also receive emails that you don't want—particularly from spammers. Spammers often guess at email addresses, so for instance they often send messages to sales@yourdomain.com or webmaster@yourdomain.com.

Google gives you the choice (see Figure 2.36) to either receive all emails addressed to your domain or to receive only those that have addresses.

Setting Up New Users

Once you have set up the email, then you can create new users. By setting up a user account, you create an email account and give the new user full access to all of the tools. As you can see in Figure 2.37, it is quite easy to set up a new user account; all you need to do is put in:

- The user's first name

- The user's last name

- The user name, which will be used when they log in and will become their email address

You put in the details, note the temporary password, click Create New User, and you're there. The new user has been created! Tell them their user name and password, and they will be good to go.

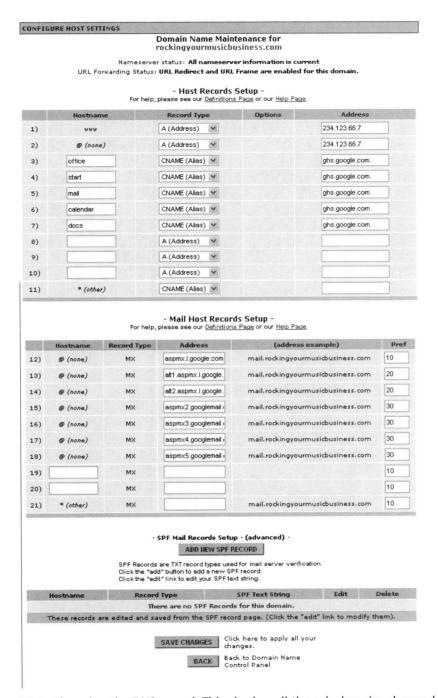

Figure 2.34 Changing the DNS record. This also has all the sub-domains changed, plus the email settings too (which will be discussed in a moment).

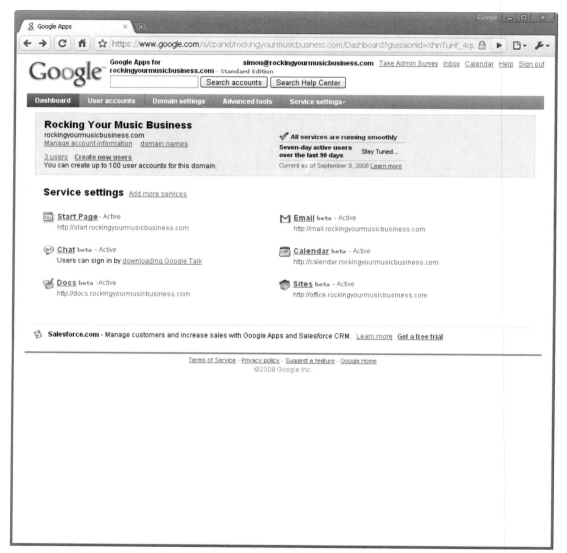

Figure 2.35 Once your sub-domains have been set up and your domain has been veri-fied, your dashboard will look something like this.

Anyone designated as administrator can see all of the users (see Figure 2.38) and can delete them as and when necessary. This means that you can grant someone temporary access, share a limited amount of information with them within the tightly controlled confines of your personalized Google office, and once they are done, delete them so

Figure 2.36 Google email settings: Among other things, Google allows you to set up a catch-all email facility.

they have no further access. This might be useful if your business is being audited—you can give your accountant access for the project and then shut him or her out at the end.

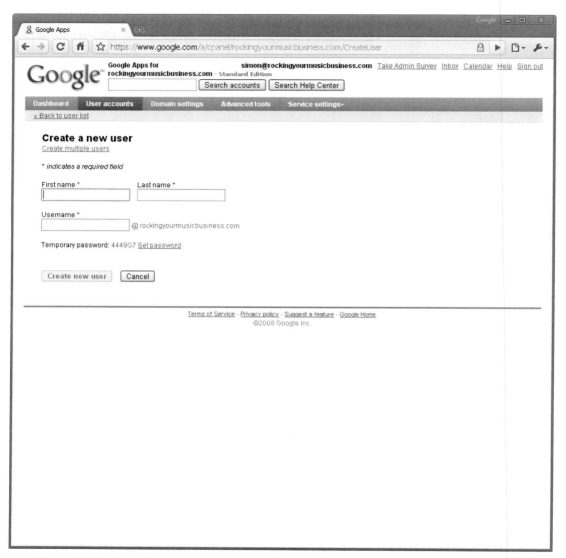

Figure 2.37   Creating a new user account in Google Apps.

Figure 2.38   Managing user accounts.

What's Next?

What's next? Nothing. Your office is up and running; you can go and run your business. You can, of course, add and remove people as and when needed, and if you want to close the whole thing down, that only needs a button click, too.

3 Working with Other People

Even if you're a solo performer, music is never a solitary activity. You will always need other people involved, whether they be collaborating musicians, sound/lighting people, or managers (to give a few examples).

Whenever you get more than one person involved, there will be differing expectations and differing understandings. For musical collaborators these differences can often lead to the creation of something totally new that none of the collaborators could create on his or her own. For business collaborators, differences can often lead to disagreements and arguments. While a business disagreement about strategy may lead to healthy discussions, a business disagreement about how much you should have been paid for that gig you played last month—in other words, a disagreement that arises after you have paid all your expenses—would not be welcomed.

To stop these sorts of disagreements—which can and do escalate into court battles—it is important that you:

- Develop a common understanding before you agree to do business.

- Ensure that this common agreement is understood by all parties and that all parties intend to be bound by the agreement.

- Record the agreement to help confirm the understanding and to ensure that everyone knows the full extent of what has been agreed upon, and so that other parties can follow the agreement.

- Change the agreement if circumstances change, the agreement is not working as intended, or there are unintended consequences.

And how do you do this? By writing it down (see Figure 3.1). Contracts may seem tedious—and to a large extent, they do lack excitement—however, I would rather spend a few hours reading a piece of paper to ensure my rights are protected and that my collaborators and I are on the same page, than lose money or spend several years in litigation (or both).

Figure 3.1 The basic tools for a contract.

The choice is yours.

In this chapter, I look at the issues you need to consider, and I have also included sample wording to illustrate how you could document some of these issues. You are quite welcome to take these words and use them as the basis of any contract. Some you can use as drafted, and some will need to be adapted. However, please do be aware that these words are offered to illustrate the points I am raising in this book—they should in no way be considered as legal advice, and you should always consider consulting a suitable qualified *and experienced* lawyer before entering into any business contract. In short, if it ever goes wrong, don't blame me and don't blame the publisher.

Band Partnership Agreement: Considerations

In many ways, the most basic, and yet the most fundamental, document is the band agreement (see Figure 3.2). In spite of this, many bands continue without one. So if you can continue without one, why bother with the hassle, effort, and arguments to draw one up, not to mention the expense? There are lots of reasons, so let me outline a few.

Figure 3.2 A band partnership agreement—it's just a stack of paper.

When Do You Need a Band Agreement?

In essence, by forming a band you are establishing a partnership. (See Chapter 1 for an explanation about the different business structures that are available.) Establishing a partnership is usually a good thing, and something that you are likely to want to do.

However, in most jurisdictions, there are overriding provisions that apply to partnerships (see Figure 3.3), which you may not want to apply to you. For instance, if someone leaves the band, then you are likely to be required to dissolve the partnership and

---

STATUTORY INSTRUMENTS

2001 No. 969

PARTNERSHIP
LIMITED LIABILITY PARTNERSHIPS

The Limited Liability Partnerships (Fees) (No. 2) Regulations 2001

Approved by both Houses of Parliament

Made - - - - -	*14th March 2001*
Laid before Parliament	*14th March 2001*
Coming into force - -	*6th April 2001*

The Secretary of State, in exercise of the powers conferred on him by section 708(1) and (2) of the Companies Act 1985(**a**), as applied to limited liability partnerships by regulation 4 of and Schedule 2 to the Limited Liability Partnerships Regulations 2001(**b**), hereby makes the following Regulations:

1. These Regulations may be cited as the Limited Liability Partnerships (Fees) (No. 2) Regulations 2001.

2. These Regulations revoke the Limited Liability Partnerships (Fees) Regulations 2001(**c**).

3. Regulations 1 and 2 shall come into force on the day after these Regulations are made. The remainder of these regulations shall come into force on 6th April 2001.

4. In these Regulations:

"the 1985 Act" means the Companies Act 1985 and any reference to a numbered section is a reference to a section of that Act;

"the 2000 Act" means the Limited Liability Partnerships Act 2000(**d**) and any reference to a numbered section is a reference to a section of that Act;

"an annual return" means a document required to be submitted by a limited liability partnership to the registrar of companies under section 363 of the 1985 Act as applied to limited liability partnerships by the Limited Liability Partnerships Regulations 2001;

"the Companies Acts" has the meaning contained in section 744 of the 1985 Act as extended by regulation 4 of the Limited Liability Partnerships Regulations 2001;

"the register" means the register kept by the registrar of companies for the purposes of the Companies Acts.

(**a**) 1985 c. 6.
(**b**) S.I. 2001/1090.
(**c**) S.I. 2001/529.
(**d**) 2000 c. 12.

1

Figure 3.3 There are huge amounts of laws governing partnerships: Here's one page of U.K. legislation, and already you're falling asleep.

establish a new one, even though it would be easier to maintain a partnership but with a different member. In short, by drawing up an agreement, you get the chance to run the band (and the partnership) in the way you want it run, not in the way someone else wants it run.

Perhaps the most pressing reason for a formal agreement is clarity. Without an agreement, how do you distinguish between being a bunch of individuals who occasionally make music together and being a band? If there's no agreement, how do you distinguish who has been hired to play a gig? How do you say, "I'm part of the band," if there is nothing to record who or what constitutes the band? If there is no "band," then the booker would be responsible for hiring all of the members individually—a mad situation that no booker would seriously contemplate.

Without an agreement—whether verbal or written—you're just a bunch of individuals.

Beyond recording who is in and who is out of the band, an agreement gives authority for the individuals to behave as a band—in other words, to behave as a single entity. For instance, when you operate as a single entity, you can authorize one person—on behalf of everyone—to:

- Book gigs
- Book studio time
- Organize CD pressing and uploading your latest album to iTunes and the other online retailers

Of course, you don't need an agreement for someone to physically upload tracks—pirates do it every day—but you do need some sort of structure to acknowledge how your intellectual property rights (in other words, your music) will be exploited (turned into cash).

When Don't You Need an Agreement?

Clearly, there are situations when you don't need a band agreement. The most obvious time that you don't need an agreement is when you are a solo performer and—since you are "the act"—you are hiring everyone else. So if you think you're in a band but there's no agreement, beware that someone else may think you're a hired hand (even if you're a hired hand who hasn't been paid). Without a written agreement, you will have difficulty disputing this interpretation.

Equally, if the band is legally constituted as a company, rather than a partnership, then you don't need an agreement. However, in these circumstances, the provisions governing how the band will act will be included in the company's constitution.

The Band Partnership Agreement in Detail

The next section includes an example band partnership agreement that you could consider as a basis for your band agreement. Before you get too carried away with pulling the agreement together, here are a few points you may wish to consider.

First, there is a general legal principle with these sorts of documents: You are only authorized to operate within the terms of your agreement. Let me give you an example—take something simple, but vital: a bank account.

It is perfectly legal to operate a bank account—there are no laws stopping it (although clearly, some religions take a view about interest, but that is not a matter for this book). However, if your agreement does not permit you to open a bank account, but you do, then whoever opens the account will be in breach of the terms of the agreement and will not have the authority (and protections) granted by the agreement to do so. When you open a bank account, the bank will ask for your authority to open an account—if you say that you have the authority, but the agreement does not grant that authority, then you have misrepresented your position to the bank. Taken to the extreme, this is fraud.

Therefore, although you may be doing something very simple and straightforward, which is within the laws of your country and is for the best possible interests of all involved, you could be committing a criminal offense if you do something you do not have the authority to undertake.

For this reason, it is important that your agreement allows you to undertake the necessary actions to run your business, and it is also necessary that there is a provision to amend the agreement so that you can include terms if you later find you need to do more than you originally intended.

Voting/Exercise of Power

One issue you are going to have to think about in some detail is how many people need to undertake an action and how many need to be involved in any decision. Some decisions don't need much thought, but others—such as the decision to expel a band member—probably need more consideration and probably warrant having everyone involved in the decision.

There are no right and wrong answers here; however, for any decision/exercise of power, these are the main options:

- One person can make the decision/undertake the action. For instance, one person can decide on his or her own to spend up to $100 of the band's money.

- Two people acting together can make a decision. For instance, two people can decide to spend up to $1,000 of the band's money.

- A simple majority is required to make a decision. (A simple majority is at least half of those eligible to be included, so if there are nine people, you would need five to make a decision.) For instance, a simple majority can decide to buy a van to get to gigs.

- A super majority (such as two-thirds or three-quarters) is required for a decision. For instance, two-thirds of band members may be required to be present at any band meeting.

- A unanimous decision less one (in other words, everyone with the exception of one person is required to make a decision). For instance, a unanimous decision less one person is required to expel a member from the band.

- A unanimous decision on which everyone needs to agree. For instance, you may require a unanimous decision to admit a new band member.

Parties to the Agreement

It is important to identify the individuals who are working as a band. The usual form is by recording their name (real name, not stage name) and their address.

Background

The background section sets out the name of the band and the name of the partnership. It also records the jurisdiction that governs the agreement. The jurisdiction will determine which courts will consider any disputes. However, you should remember that just because you have established your band partnership agreement under a particular country or state's jurisdiction, that does not mean all of your disputes will be governed by that jurisdiction's laws: Each contract you enter into (for instance, with a management company or to play a series of gigs) may be governed by a different jurisdiction.

Services and External Activities

The services and external activities section is intended to indicate:

- What is expected of each band member

- What activities band members are expected to refrain from doing

The draft agreement in the next section is quite tough in prohibiting band members from getting involved in any other musical activities. This may seem unreasonable—after all, why shouldn't someone release his or her own solo album or appear as a guest artist on another album?

Although you may find lots of activities in which you want to get involved, this issue comes down to one of focus. If you focus, then you stand a chance of succeeding. If you don't, then your chances are lower. By prohibiting external activities—especially during the early part of a band's career—you ensure that each member is 100-percent committed to the project (and if they're not, then get them out).

Income, Expenditure, and Assets

The provisions covering income, expenditure, and assets are highly significant—this is the provision to allow band assets to be paid to band members. This is how the partnership will generate income for the members, so if you pay attention to nothing else, pay attention here!

These provisions operate so that:

- All income and assets belong equally to everyone within the partnership.

- All debts are met from partnership assets, and to the extent that there are insufficient assets to meet these debts, the partners will put in cash to meet the debt in equal shares.

- Instead of cash, assets may be transferred into and out of the partnership's ownership, and in this case the asset will be valued after taking advice from someone who is qualified (by his or her experience) to offer an opinion.

As drafted, all shares are equal (so everyone will have the same income). However, you could reword this so some individuals take a larger share (which obviously means that some would take a lesser share).

The provision also limits how much may be spent without authorization. There are three tiers of spending:

- Up to $100, which requires no authorization (so any band member could authorize)

- Up to $1,000, which requires two members to agree

- Over $1,000, which requires three-quarters of the members to agree

Ownership of Intangible Assets

The agreement sets out that the partnership owns:

- The band name

- Any related internet domains

- The band logo

You could include other intangible assets, such as the mailing list. Although no one is likely to argue about a mailing list, it would have a lot of value for a departing band member.

Proceedings of the Band Members

Provisions are included to detail how the band members will operate when they meet. These provisions include voting majorities and quorum requirements (the number of people needed before meeting attendees can make a decision about band business).

Accounts and Records

Chapter 5 deals with accounts in more detail, but we'll discuss them for a moment here.

Accounts are hugely significant for each band member because they determine:

- What each individual earns from the band

- The value of the business (from which each band member will be able to see the share of the value that he or she owns)

Without accurate records, a member's income or asset value will be wrong, so the provisions require that accounts are drawn up promptly on an annual basis and are then audited by a suitably qualified auditor.

Professional Advice

The band is permitted to take advice from suitably qualified professional individuals, such as lawyers or accountants. Where they may want to take advice from someone who is not regulated by a recognized professional body—for instance, they may wish to take advice about the value of some musical instruments when one member leaves—they may consult someone who has sufficient experience to be able to give a competent opinion.

Appointment of Agents

Within the terms of this agreement, an agent is anyone appointed to do something (anything) on behalf of the band. (For instance, the band may appoint someone to operate their bank account on their behalf.) The term "agent" is not intended to be narrowly interpreted only to mean a booking agent (or any other form of entertainment agent).

As an example, the band may appoint someone to manage their merchandise. It is important that this person has the clear authority to enter into contracts on behalf of the band—if they don't, then they won't be able to order more T-shirts.

Equally, the band may want to appoint someone to act as their "banker" and pay any money that the band owes. In this case, it is crucial that the person understands what they can and cannot pay for. It is even more important that they then report back to the band.

Disputes and Arbitration

The band is given power to settle their disputes between the members. However, there will be times when this is not practical—in these events, the provisions require the dispute to be submitted to arbitration.

Unlike a court, which is intended to be a neutral forum where the judge rules, in arbitration, the arbitrator will actively try to help each party reach a compromise. Usually this leads to a solution that is more acceptable to both parties. Much more importantly, it usually leads to much lower legal fees.

Amendment

Provision has been included to allow the agreement to be amended. This is intended to allow the band to make changes to reflect future business considerations and situations that arise after the agreement was drawn up.

Joining and Leaving the Band

A new member may join—and so become a partner—with the unanimous decision of the other band members. On joining, the new member will be required to buy his or her share of the business. While this may seem harsh, remember that any departing members can take their share of the assets with them, so in essence this provision is there for the new member to buy a departing member's share of the business.

Remember, just because someone joins the performing band, they don't have to become a full partner—you could simply hire the person as a freelance musician.

A band member will leave the band:

- If the remaining band members unanimously decide.

- Upon death. This is not as daft as it sounds: This provision makes it clear that the deceased member's heirs are only entitled to his or her share of the assets, not to become band members/partners of the business in his or her place.

- Upon the member giving notice to the other members.

On leaving, the ex-member will be due his or her share of the assets. In addition, if there is any future income in which the departing member has an interest—for instance, income arising from sound recording or publishing—this will continue to be paid unless the remaining members buy out this liability (in other words, pay a cash sum to extinguish the obligation to make further payments).

Transfer of Interest

The agreement prohibits any individual from transferring or selling his or her interest. This could prevent your drummer from gambling his share of the partnership in a poker game or the guitarist from losing her share in a messy divorce.

Warranties and Indemnities

The warranties are intended so that each band member can confirm that he or she is a suitable individual to enter into a business arrangement. Provisions are then included that if any member misrepresents his or her position (or takes any action to harm the band), he or she will be (personally) liable for any losses incurred as a result of these actions.

Termination of This Band Partnership Agreement

This band partnership agreement will be terminated if a majority of band members decide to do so. The termination provision sets out how the assets will be divided. The provisions also limit the use of the band's name, any URLs, and any logos—this limitation is suggested to ensure that no member then tries to immediately trade on the band's reputation.

What the Agreement Does Not Cover

This agreement does not cover:

- Ownership of recorded material

- Publishing

In both cases, I am assuming that these issues will be dealt with by external contracts. However, if they are not, then you may include them under the list of intangible assets. If you do this, then these will be regarded as assets of the whole band. Although this approach may be suitable for recordings, if only one or two members of the band are responsible for songwriting, these individuals may wish to reserve their rights.

They may also wish to reserve the income stream that flows from these rights. That being said, with some bands the songwriters retain their rights but share the income while the band is still active, since the income from the rights primarily flows as a result of the band's activities.

In the event that assets that generate a future stream of income are included within the band agreement (such as publishing rights), when a member leaves you can either:

- Try to ascribe a value to those future earnings. Typically, this will involve estimating how much will be earned.

- Continue to pay the individual for his or her future earnings (as has been suggested in the draft agreement).

Band Partnership Agreement: Example Wording

This Band Partnership Agreement is made on [date] between:

1.   [name] of [address]

2.   [name] of [address], and

3.   [name] of [address]

These individuals are collectively known as the Band and individually as the Band Members.

Background

The Band Members have determined to form a band known as [band name] which will operate as a partnership known as [partnership name]. [Geographical jurisdiction] law governs this agreement.

This agreement records the basis on which the individuals will work together and will come into force on [date].

Services and External Activities

Each Band Member shall provide all necessary services to the partnership in order that the Band can fulfill its obligations. Such services shall include, but not be limited to:

- Performing in connection with sound recordings

- Performing in all media (including radio, visual, and on stage), and

- Promoting the Band and its business.

Band Members are not be permitted to engage in any musical entertainment activities which are not related to the activities of the Band and its business.

Income, Expenditure, and Assets

All income (whether in cash or in kind) generated from any Band activity shall be an asset of the Band.

The Band may from time to time acquire such assets as a majority of the Band Members deem necessary for the performance of its business. The Band may dispose of assets from time to time as decided by a majority of the Band Members. If any asset is to be acquired from or sold to one of the Band Members, then the value of the asset shall be determined by a unanimous decision of the Band Members after taking advice from a qualified valuer.

All costs, charges, and expenses incurred in connection with the Band and its business shall be met out of the assets of the Band. Any single expense over $100 shall require the prior authorization of at least two Band Members. Any single expense over $1,000 shall require the prior authorization of at least three-quarters of the Band Members.

The Band shall pay any tax (direct, indirect, and arising from any jurisdiction), for which the partnership may be liable, from the assets of the Band.

All capital shall belong to the Band Members equally. In the event that there is insufficient capital to meet any expense, the Band Members shall each contribute an equal amount to meet this cost. Subject to the unanimous agreement of all Band Members, a part of the capital may be paid to the Band Members, and each Band Member shall receive an equal payment (before tax or any other deductions).

Contributions and payments may be made in assets, in which case the value of any assets shall be determined by the unanimous decision of the Band Members, having taken advice from a qualified valuer if necessary.

Bank Accounts

The Band shall open and maintain such bank accounts as a majority of the Band Members agree to be necessary.

Insurance

The Band may take out such insurance as a majority of the Band Members deem necessary. The expense of any insurance shall be an expense to be met by the assets of the partnership.

Ownership on Intangible Assets

The partnership shall own the following:

- The Band name: [band name]

- The following internet domains: [URLs associated with the band]

- The band logo: [attach a copy or include specifications to identify any logos]

Proceedings of the Band Members

a.   The Band Members shall meet at such times and at such places as they decide and shall make regulations for the conduct of their business, for the appointment of a secretary and for all other matters in connection with execution of business under this agreement. The chair at any meeting of the Band Members shall be chosen by the Band Members present at that meeting.

b.   Two of the Band Members present at any meeting of the Band Members of which two weeks' notice has been given to all Band Members shall form a quorum. Each question arising shall be decided by a simple majority of the votes of the Band Members, except where there are only two Band Members present at a meeting, when any decision must be unanimous. In the event that there is an equality of votes, the chair of the meeting shall have a second or casting vote. In the event of an equality of votes on the election of the chair, the Band Member to take the chair shall be chosen by lot.

c.   A resolution in writing signed by a majority of the Band Members (or both Band Members if there are only two), but of which notice has been given to all of the Band Members individually, shall be as valid and effectual as if it had been passed at a meeting of the Band Members, and the resolution may consist of one or more documents in similar form.

d.   In any event, the Band Members shall meet once every year for the purpose of agreeing the Band's accounts.

Accounts and Records

The Band Members shall keep such accounts and records (including electronic records), and employ such persons as are necessary to keep such accounts and records, as may be appropriate for the proper working of this Band Partnership Agreement. The accounts and records shall be made available to any Band Member at any reasonable time.

The Band's financial year shall end on [day/month]. The Band Members shall ensure that accounts are prepared promptly after the end of the financial year.

These accounts shall be audited by an auditor with a suitable professional qualification within three months of the end of the financial year.

The audited accounts shall be sent to all Band Members within 30 days of being signed by the auditor.

Professional Advice

The Band Members may from time to time, on a decision made by a majority of the Band Members, appoint a lawyer, an auditor, and such other professional persons on such terms as to remuneration and otherwise as the Band Members think fit. In the event that the Band requires advice from an individual for whom there is no recognized professional body, then they shall appoint someone who by their experience appears to have the competence to give the appropriate advice.

Appointment of Agents

On a decision made by a majority of Band Members, the Band may:

a.   employ agents in the transaction of any business; and

b.   authorize that checks and other documents be signed by one or more of their number or by such other person or persons as they may appoint for this purpose.

The appointment, which shall include details of any remuneration or fees, shall be made in writing.

Disputes and Arbitration

The Band Members shall settle all questions or disputes arising as to the meaning of any provision of this Agreement.

In the event of any dispute between the Band Members and/or any former Band Members, the Band Members may settle, compromise, or submit to arbitration any claims or matters relating to the rights of the individuals in question.

Amendment

Subject to the agreement of all of the Band Members less one, the Band Members may at any time alter any of the provisions of this Agreement. Any such alteration may have retrospective effect, but no amendment may retrospectively reduce any individual's entitlement under this Band Partnership Agreement without his or her approval.

Joining and Leaving the Band

With the unanimous decision of the other Band Members, an individual may join the Band and so become a Band Member and subject to the terms of this Band Partnership Agreement. This shall be confirmed in writing by an agreement signed by all of the Band Members including the joining Band Member.

Immediately before joining the Band, the existing Band Members shall determine the current value of the Band's assets. The new Band Member shall then pay a sum (in cash or assets) equivalent to one person's share of the assets.

A Band Member shall leave the Band:

a.   if the remaining Band Members unanimously decide

b.   on death, or

c.   on the expiry of three months' notice to quit which shall be given to the other Band Members.

On leaving the Band, the departing Band Member shall be entitled to an appropriate share of the Band's assets, taking account of the current assets and liabilities of the Band. The departing Band Member's share may be paid in cash or in assets as determined by the remaining Band Members. In the event that any amounts are paid in assets, these shall be valued at a fair market value as determined by the Band Members having taken advice from a suitably experienced valuer.

In addition, any departing Band Member shall continue to be eligible for their share of any income that is paid on an ongoing basis that arises from any sound recording or publishing rights and which the departing Band Member would have been entitled to if he or she had not left, unless that individual confirms in writing that he or she has no such further expectations.

Transfer of Interest

No interest in the partnership may be sold or transferred to another individual without the agreement of all Band Members.

Warranties and Indemnities

In entering into this partnership agreement, each Band Member confirms and warrants:

■   [He/she] is free to enter into this agreement and is under no other obligations that would conflict with [his/her] obligations under this agreement.

- [He/she] has no personal debt (except any that have been disclosed in writing to the other Band Members).

- [He/she] will take no action which brings the Band's reputation into disrepute and which would cause the Band to be unable to fulfill any of its obligations.

Each Band Member indemnifies the other Band Members against any claim arising from any breach of these warranties.

Termination of this Band Partnership Agreement

This Band Partnership Agreement shall be terminated if a majority of Band Members together decide.

Upon the termination of this Band Partnership Agreement:

a. The Band Members shall meet all outstanding costs, charges, and expenses from the assets of the Band.

b. Once all liabilities of the Band have been met, the remaining assets of the Band shall be distributed equally between the Band Members in such manner that the Band Members may agree. In the event that the Band Members cannot agree on an equitable split, then any non-cash assets of the Band shall be sold and the remaining sums shall be distributed.

c. Unless there has been agreement by at least three-quarters of the Band, then no Band Member shall use the Band's name, associated internet domains, and the logo for a period of at least 24 months from the termination of the Band.

Signed

_____

Member 1

_____

Member 2

_____

Member 3

_____

Gigs

Live performances are a fundamental part of any musician's business. Indeed, for many musicians the live performance is why they are in the music business, and without that connection with people, there is nothing. If you want to know the details about what you need to do organize a tour, then you should check out *The Tour Book* by Andy Reynolds (Thomson Course Technology PTR, 2007), which is an excellent book that will tell you everything you need to know.

For this book, I will only cover the contractual issues—and then, only the issues that matter. If you want to go wild and start imposing riders (you know, chocolate flamingos in the dressing room for each band member, no red M&Ms within 25 meters of the stage, and so on), then feel free. I'm not going to put that advice here.

As far as the contractual issues go, there are certain key issues you may need to agree upon:

- When you are playing—date and time on stage.

- The address of the venue at which you are playing.

- When you can set up and check the sound.

- The number of performers.

- Who is being contracted to play and what is expected (in terms of set content and length).

- How much and when you will be paid.

- What you have to provide and what is provided (in particular, PA, lights, door/security staff, and so on).

- What liability you are taking on (for instance, who will be required to have public liability insurance in place). You may want to try to cover your equipment by the venue's insurance while your equipment is within the venue—however, most venues will resist these provisions (although they are likely to be obligated to carry public liability insurance).

Example Gig Contract

There is no need for complicated contracts—gig contracts just need to cover all of the points noted above that are relevant. The contract could look like this (although after you have played a few gigs, you will probably want to tweak this a bit and develop your own "standard" document):

This contract is made on [date] between [gig booker/venue of address] and [band name of address].

[The band] will perform at [the venue/full address] on [day date], a set lasting approximately [time] starting at [time]. The set will include [brief description of set] and there will be [number] performers on stage.

Access to the venue is available from [time] and sound checking may be undertaken from [time] on the day of the performance.

The total fee for the performance is [$] . [$] will be paid by [date] by way of deposit, with the balance being due on completion of the performance. If the deposit is not paid by the specified date, then the band shall have the right to terminate this agreement without incurring any liability or obligation.

The venue will provide lights and public address system, and shall be responsible for the safety of everyone at the venue.

Signed

_____   _____

On behalf of the band   On behalf of the venue/booking agent

Working with Other Musicians

There are so many opportunities for confusion when you are working with other musicians. The key confusions that may arise (and so should be stamped on swiftly and firmly) are:

- The expectations of income and future employment. Musicians need to understand whether they are being asked to provide a one-off performance (perhaps for a recording) or whether they are being contracted to supply services on a regular basis—perhaps as musicians on a tour.

- If the musician is being asked to become a regular performer, then it should be clear whether he or she is joining as an employee or as a partner to the band. In other words, will he be an employee with a salary (which may have bonuses attached) or will he be sharing in the ownership and profits as a partner.

- The role that the musician played in the creation of a piece. If you want a tin whistle part on one of your songs and you get a player in, it is important that the player understands that he is there as a player and is not expected to contribute as a songwriter, and hence, his total fee will be what he is paid, and there will be no future royalties. Of course, if the player does create something new, and you want to use it, then the contract should be amended.

■ The agreement that the performance (if recorded) may be used commercially (see the upcoming "Recordings" section).

These are all, in essence, matters of clarity.

Live Performances

For live performances, it is key that any agreement specifies:

■ What is expected (for instance, "You will play bass").

■ When the gig begins, how long it lasts, and what time the musician is expected to arrive.

■ Whether there are any special requirements (perhaps for gear or costumes).

■ How much the musician will be paid.

Also, if the performance is to be recorded, then any recording issues are also relevant.

Recordings

If you are hiring a musician for recording, then clearly he needs to know where he needs to be, the time he needs to be there, and what you want him to bring (in terms of instruments). In addition, you will also need the musician to sign a release confirming that he agrees that his performance may be commercially released. Most record labels will not agree to music being made commercially available without a release from all the musicians on a project.

This release could take the following form:

This release agreement is made between [musician name and address] and [the Band] in connection with the performance by the musician.

The musician will be paid [$] for his/her performance. This performance has been recorded (in addition to performances by the band). In consideration of the payment, the musician assigns all rights in connection with the performance to the band (and these rights may be further reassigned by the band).

In the event of any dispute that the musician and the band cannot settle, the matter shall be submitted to a mutually agreed mediator. If a solution cannot be reached through mediation, then the matter shall be submitted to arbitration at a venue determined by the band.

This agreement constitutes the entire understanding between the musician and the band and does not confer any rights on the musician.

Signed

_____   _____

On behalf of the musician   On behalf of the band

Manager

Any manager is likely to want to put forward his or her own contract, and then there may be an amount of negotiation. Accordingly, it is probably more important that you have thought about the key negotiating points rather than approach a business arrangement by asking the manager to sign your document.

Money

There are two key issues in any management contract: what you pay and what the manager does for that money.

Most managers charge around 20 percent. It is unlikely that you will be able to change the percentage by much—however, you may be able to negotiate about how the 20 percent is applied. Typically, managers charge 20 percent of the gross income of the band, and then charge expenses in addition.

Gross income is your total income—that is your income before any deductions. So if you play a gig and get paid $100, your gross income is $100, so your manager gets paid $20 (assuming he is taking 20 percent). Now, let's say it costs you $50 in gas to drive to the gig and $60 to hire a sound system. You've now earned $100 but spent $110, and so your manager takes... that's right, $20, because he takes 20 percent of the gross earnings; see Table 3.1.

In short, your manager could make a profit when you make a loss. More than that, his profit could make your loss even worse—in this example, you would have to reach in your pocket and find $20 out of your own resources to pay him for the privilege of playing the gig (in addition to the $10 you have already lost).

Most managers understand this dilemma and will limit their cut when you are not making any profit. However, you need to go beyond this and ensure that both sides understand what is included within gross earnings. For instance, if the record label pays tour support (in other words, pays for you to be included as the support act on a tour), should your manager take 20 percent of that?

Table 3.1 Paying Your Manager

Income	Expenditure
Income from gig	$100
Gas to get to gig	$50
Sound-system hire	$60
Manager's fee	$20
Total earnings (well, loss)	$130

Equally, there are considerations as to what the manager's fee should include. For instance, should it include earnings from publishing? Should it include earnings from publishing if only one person writes the songs?

Beyond that, what other expenses can the manager charge? For instance, if he comes to see you perform at a gig, can he charge his travelling expenses to the band? Can he also charge hotel or other accommodation expenses? There is no right or wrong answer, but you do need to understand what you are paying before you pay it, and equally, you may want to limit the expenses that can be incurred (for instance, explicitly state that expenses charged may not exceed $1,000 in any month).

Obligations and Duties

Most bands don't mind paying their manager 20 percent, provided he makes them money. Accordingly, it is important to express the key duties and obligations of the manager. There are likely to be three or four areas where the manager can help the band, and to an extent these overlap.

Finding Work

Perhaps the main role for any manager will be to find work for a band—or rather, not work, but opportunities to exploit the band's assets (its intellectual property). The manager should not simply look for opportunities, but he should help to create them (for instance, by setting up a tour or looking at how a recording could be licensed).

The manager should try to ensure the band is working to its maximum capacity and is generating as much income as possible.

Contract Negotiation

In order to work, the band will need to enter into a lot of contracts. These may be contracts with record labels, gig promoters, merchandisers, and so on. The manager will need to stay on top of each contract and negotiate on behalf of the band.

Once a contract is in place, the manager should then seek to ensure that it generates the intended income for the band (and himself).

Running the Business

One task you may want your manager to undertake is running your business, in effect becoming the chief executive of your business. This has many advantages, including the efficiency of having everything in one place—nothing will fall between the cracks between your manager and your business (theoretically).

However, it also has disadvantages; for instance, your business is highly dependent on your manager, and the infrastructure of your business would likely be taken over by him. If your manager ceases to act, then you would not only have to find a new manager, but you could have to rebuild your whole business and infrastructure. Also, if your manager is focusing on running your business, he won't be focusing on finding you new business.

Many bands have separate personal managers and business managers. There is good sense in this approach, but you need to ensure it works to further your career and your business before you adopt this practice.

Guidance and Advice

Another key role for the manager is giving advice to the band to further their career and increase their earnings. Much of this advice will have an impact on what work and what contracts the manager then negotiates on behalf of the band.

Term of the Contract

An important decision is how long the management contract should last. In looking at the length of the contract, you should differentiate between the length of the contract and the length of your relationship with your manager—it is quite possible, indeed in some cases common, to renew a contract when a previous one ends. This can give the opportunity to revise and update any provisions that may no longer be appropriate.

The most straightforward term of a contract would be set as a number of years—perhaps the contract ends two or three years after signing. However, you may want the contract to end sooner, for instance:

- If the band does not earn a certain minimum income, you may then want the contract to end.

- If the band does not increase its earnings (either by a certain amount or by a certain percentage) on a year-to-year basis, then you might want the contract to end.

- If the manager fails to secure (or maintain) a suitable contract, you may want the contract to end. Primarily, this would be for a major-label record deal, but you may want to end the contract if other deals cannot be reached.

Post-Term Payments

One reason for giving a manager a long-term contract is to give him an incentive to work hard. If the contract is too short and he can't see how he could make money during that short period, then the manager is unlikely to want to work with you. Equally, some deals take a long time to set up; it may then be a long time before the resulting income-generating event happens, and it may be even longer before the income is then received. Think about a major tour—that may take six months to set up, there may be another three to six months before the tour starts, the tour may last for eighteen months, and it may take another six months after the end of the tour before all the income has been collected.

This could mean that it might take three years from the moment the idea of the tour is conceived until when the income is received. If you're a manager with a two-year contract, why would you bother working on this project? You could work for two years and then the money comes in during the third year, after your contract has ended. Even for more modest projects, much of the work that a manager does today will not see any income for several years.

One approach a manager could take would be not to start any project that may only bring income after the end of a contract. Clearly, this would not be beneficial to either side. The alternative is to agree how income generated during the period of the contract will be paid after the contract has ended. There are two approaches you could take here:

- Continue to pay the manager his percentage for any deal negotiated during his tenure. Therefore, if he negotiated an album deal and a tour, he would continue to receive income from these albums and the tour.

- Continue to pay the manager a percentage based on all (pre-termination) business, but have this decline over a period of time. So for instance, if the manager is paid 20 percent, then you may pay:
  - Twenty percent for earnings during the first year after the contract ends
  - Fifteen percent for earnings during the second year after the contract ends
  - Ten percent for earnings during the third year after the contract ends
  - Five percent for earnings during the fourth year after the contract ends

Usually the second approach is favored because it gives a clear indication of when the financial relationship between the two parties ends.

Whichever approach is taken, a key issue is to ensure that any income earned from deals struck after the contract has ended (in other words, deals brought in by a new manager) would be outside the scope of this approach, unless the old manager had done a significant amount of work in connection with a deal. For instance, if he negotiated a new record contract that was signed the day after his contract ended, then it might be reasonable to include that as a deal stuck during his tenure.

Staff

You may need staff for a range of different functions, and the length of time that you will engage an individual will differ depending on the function he or she fulfills. For instance, you may need someone to open the mail and reply to all your fan mail—this sort of person would likely be a permanent employee who you retain for as long as the band is in existence. Alternatively, you might hire a chef to come on the road with you—in this instance, the contract would last as long as the tour, and at the end, the chef would need to look for new employment.

You should also remember that there are different ways you can hire people—particularly if you need people to help with administrative tasks. With the internet it is a simple task to hire someone on the other side of the world who lives in a low-cost location. Clearly, though, this approach would not be appropriate if you are looking for a roadie to look after your guitars while you are on tour.

Remote Workers

If you are looking for someone to do an hour or two of administrative work each day—perhaps you want that person to answer emails and make a few calls to confirm gigs or chase down suppliers—then the option of a remote worker might be appealing and would have many advantages. One of the key advantages is cost—you can, quite literally, hire someone to work for a few dollars. This may feel like exploitation, but often these levels of salary can be quite good in comparison to the available salaries in the individual's location.

Also, you will often find it easier to hire a remote worker to do a few hours of work here than you would to hire someone locally to work for an hour or two here and there. When you hire a person to work in your physical office, they will usually only have one job—the job you have hired them to perform. They will therefore expect a regular wage regardless of whether there is work to do, so you may find yourself looking for jobs for them to do. However, if you are hiring a remote worker, that person will usually understand that the work from any one individual will vary with demand, and accordingly, they will usually have several clients to balance out their workflow, so the amount of work they can do for you can expand and contract based on your needs.

If you have set up your office in the cloud (see Chapter 2), then you will already be set up to have someone work remotely with you.

There are several websites dedicated to helping employers and contractors get in touch. One of the bigger names in this market is Elance (elance.com). One challenge with these sites is trying to figure out who is any good—some sites give ratings, but these are often not particularly helpful. A far more practical approach is to try someone on a small task. If the person is any good, then you can use him or her again and start to build a relationship. As both parties' confidence grows, you can use your new staff member more regularly and integrate him or her as a member of your team.

With remote workers there are only a few key issues that you need to agree upon between you:

- What they are going to do for you

- When they are going to finish the task

- How much you are going to pay them

- When you are going to pay them

It is in the interest of both parties that all of these matters are agreed upon up front.

If you then expand the role of the individual (or group of individuals—quite often there are advantages to working with a firm of remote workers), then both sides need to ensure that there is a clear understanding about what will be done and when it will be done. When you hire someone for a single job, then it is easy to specify what has to be achieved. If you're looking for someone to do something on an ongoing basis—for instance, reply to your emails—this is harder. Take the example of responding to emails: You would have to think about how often emails should be checked, how quickly the response should be sent, whether you should be consulted, and so on.

Also, if you are hiring a remote worker on an ongoing basis, you need to be clear about the expectations on both sides, both from a legal and from a practical purpose. If the other person believes he or she is an employee and has made future plans based on that understanding, that then places an obligation on you (even if only a moral obligation) to consider his or her interests when you make decisions.

Hiring Individuals in Person

There will be times when you want to hire a specific person to undertake a specific task. Indeed, this is likely to be the most common form of hiring for most bands. For instance, you will probably want to hire technicians for your live performances—in these instances, you are likely to want specific people with specific skills, whose work you trust.

Before you hire someone, I recommend you consult an employment lawyer. He or she will be able to advise you about the latest legislative and practical developments and will be able to ensure that you do everything right, so you don't create liabilities or take on responsibilities that you were not expecting. A lawyer will also be able to talk about jurisdiction and the implications of hiring people in different locations.

Employees

When you hire someone, you typically hire that person as an employee. In most jurisdictions, there are several implications that flow from hiring employees in this manner:

- Employment law directly applies to the relationship. This gives the employee certain rights (for instance, to notice of termination and to pursue claims through the employment courts).

- As employer, you will usually be required to deduct income tax from the employee's wages before you pay his or her salary. You may also be required to make other deductions—for instance, for statutory social costs or if the wages have been garnished (perhaps for family support payments).

Independent Contractors

With an independent contractor, you are contracting for the provision of a service, not an individual to perform that service. Now clearly, if you hire a contractor who is a sole trader, then you probably have a good idea about who will provide the services.

The perceived advantages of this approach are:

- You do not have an employee, so employment law does not apply (so you don't have to give benefits such as vacation and so on).

- You are not required to deduct tax and social payments—you simply pay the amount agreed upon in the contract. In these circumstances, the contractor would then be responsible for his or her tax affairs.

However—particularly when you engage individuals—employment law can still be applied, and the individual must be treated as an employee. Whether this applies to you is highly dependent on the jurisdiction in which you are operating, so you should take legal advice. For instance, in some jurisdictions, if you employ an independent contractor for longer than one year, that person is deemed to be an employee, which gives him or her employment rights, such as the right not to have the contract unfairly terminated. This could mean that you would have to pay the employee compensation at the end of the contractual period.

Sometimes independent contractors set themselves up as companies—this often has advantages for the individual, such as the allowances they can claim for tax purposes and the limitation of liabilities. However, in certain jurisdictions the law will look through these arrangements to the underlying employment relationship. You may therefore find that even if you engage a company, you are still required to operate tax arrangements as an employer and to treat the individual as an employee.

Contractual Issues

Whenever you engage someone to work for you, whether as an employee or as an independent contractor (but particularly for employees), there are a few issues you should consider:

- The task you want the employee to perform. The task should be clear and should be within the capabilities of the individual.

- The amount of pay, which will include basic pay, any allowances, bonuses, and whether the pay is reviewed from time to time.

- Leave. In some jurisdictions you are required to give vacation leave. In many you are required to give maternity/paternity leave, too.

- The procedure to terminate the contract—in particular, the notice period that you require an employee to give you.

- The grievance procedure that should be followed. While this may seem tedious (and it is), this is one area of employment law where employers often get into difficulties. Very often employers can be in the right but lose a case because they didn't follow their own procedures.

- The location at which the work is to be performed. Clearly when you are hiring someone who will work as part of your road crew, you will need to specify that the individual works wherever you are. However, you may need other people to be mobile—for instance, you may need to have an accountant on the road with you to look after the money.

- Health and safety are significant issues. As an employer you will have all sorts of legislation applying to you, and each time you cross a state/country border, you will find a whole new raft of regulations that apply to you (and your lawyers will be happy to tell you about all the requirements). For a band on the road, there are many opportunities for things to go wrong, so you need to take this issue seriously. Equally, you need to be aware of vicarious liability—the liabilities that arise for you following the action of one or more of your employees.

■ You may not think that intellectual property issues are relevant to your staff, but that may be. You should ensure that contracts are clear that the rights to any intellectual property created by your employees are owned by the band. For instance, if someone in your office creates a logo, because they have done that "on your dime," that logo should be owned by their employer.

Without the right people, your business won't run, so it is worth taking the time to make sure the business aspects of your relationship are solid.

4 Running Your Business Online

In Chapter 2 I looked at how to set up your office. I now want to take some of those concepts further and look at how you run your business. This chapter is about the mechanics of running your business—it is not a recommendation for the areas of business you should be in. If you want to know more about my thoughts on your business and career strategy, then you should check out *Building a Successful 21st Century Music Career*.

This chapter looks at the online business aspects of your business. The real-world aspects of running your business are covered through the rest of this book.

As a first step, it's probably worth thinking about some of the tasks you can achieve online. Some things you will do online are marketing, and some things will be immediately commercial. However, where one ends and the other begins may be a difficult line to draw. So what might you do online?

- Run your office! Hopefully Chapter 2 has convinced you that at least some of your business needs to be in the cloud.

- Run your website (yeah, I know ... it's not a website if it's not online, but you can't miss this piece).

- Run your blog.

- Participate in social networking sites.

- Interact and communicate with fans.

- Run your mailing list.

- Advertise your forthcoming events (with an online calendar and links to maps, where appropriate).

- Take bookings for gigs.
- Sell merchandise.

Before we look at these in a bit more detail, it might be useful to remember a few key points:

- Anything you set up in the online world should be practical. It's no good having a brilliant system if it costs too much or if no one understands how it works, especially if the people who don't understand how it works are (1) you and your collaborators, and (2) your fan base.

- Everything you do in the online world should support your business. There's no point in doing anything just because you can and/or everyone else is doing it. That isn't to say that everything you do should make money—indeed, there's a lot to be said for doing things that are fun, altruistic, or great marketing—but when time and money are limited, you should focus on the money-raising stuff first, even if those activities raise money only in the long term.

- The point of doing online business is that it doesn't need constant human intervention. This means that your online business will be up and running all day every day, so you can be finding new fans and selling things while you are asleep, playing a gig, or doing hundreds of other things apart from being online. With this in mind, your online world needs to be understandable to anyone and everyone—explanation should not be necessary, and equally, someone whose first language is not the same as yours should be able to understand what's going on. You should make your site as simple and as logical as possible (which means you need to throw out the self-indulgent junk). So for instance, fans should be able to find when and where the next gig is, and your auditors should be able to access your expenses for last year.

- It is easy to set up some free web space, but these sites can look really cheap and nasty. It can be really expensive to set up a highly slick website. However, you can make a very small investment to move your website from that horrible "free" look to something that looks quite impressive. After that, further investment tends not to pay dividends (see Figure 4.1). Learn to stop when something is good enough. You shouldn't compromise the quality of your music, but you can cut a few corners with your website provided you have sorted the basics. Part of managing your costs is ensuring that you are using appropriate providers (such as the right web host) for your needs.

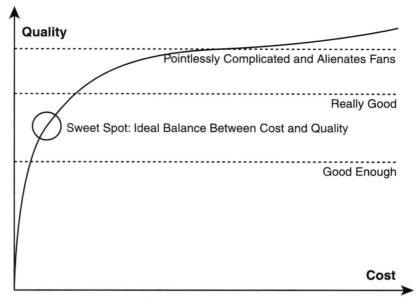

Figure 4.1   Your business is making music, so you shouldn't necessarily aim to have the best website ever seen. You need to figure out where your website is good enough and stop spending money (unless, of course, the expense brings in new fans or helps to retain your existing fans).

Website

Your website should serve one key purpose: to support your business. To provide that support, your site should:

- Interact with your fan base (and potential fans)
- Interact with, and support, your business associates

That's a lot of interaction—a lot of two-way communication, and before that communication can happen, you need to encourage people to visit, so at its most basic your website must post information about you. You can do this as:

- Text
- Music clips
- Videos

However, there is a lot more you can do with a website beyond making it look like a glorified photo gallery or jukebox. Here are a few thoughts.

Selling

In this section I'm going to talk about a lot of things you can do with your website. Let me first focus on the really important one: selling.

At the foundation of your business is commerce—you provide music and related products, and your fan base gives you money. We can debate over what those products are and how they are delivered, but the commercial nature of your venture cannot be disputed.

You could choose to only sell through offline outlets, but this could restrict your market. By selling online you have the opportunity to have your store open 24 hours a day, 7 days a week, and available to everyone around the globe. That won't guarantee any income, but it does offer a great opportunity—certainly a much better opportunity than selling to just your friends.

There are many different things you can sell and many different approaches you can adopt. This book focuses on the business aspects of music, so I suggest you check out *Building a Successful 21st Century Music Career* (this book's sibling) to read more about the strategic issues you should consider.

From a practical perspective, there are a few factors you need to focus on in order to sell from your website:

- Making the product available

- Having a means to take money

- Having the means to fulfill the order

To a large extent, these three issues may be interlinked.

Making the Product Available

There are many different products that you may wish to sell through your site. Typical examples of the range of products you may wish to sell might include:

- Gig tickets

- CDs

- Downloads

- Merchandise (such as T-shirts or mugs)

In order to sell, you need to be acutely aware of how people buy, and then make it as easy as possible for people to do so.

Let me give you an example: gig tickets. If someone comes to your site looking for the dates when you are next playing, then they will probably not look to buy tickets in the Shop section of your website. However, if all of your gig listings have links to buy tickets (even if those are links to an external ticket agency), you will encourage people to buy tickets.

By contrast, if—having told someone when you are playing—you then leave them to find a ticket outlet and hope that they don't get too distracted before they get to purchase the ticket, you are likely to lose sales. The easier you make it for people to see a product—any product—and click a button to buy, the easier it will be to generate sales. People act on impulse—allow their impulses to work in your favor.

By the way, I'm not decrying the inclusion of a Shop button—indeed, I think you should have one. My only point here is that you should link everything to sales and developing your business. So if you've got a news item about your new CD, then include a purchase link. This isn't about hard selling; it's about helping people to buy of their own free will. Make it easy for people to buy stuff, and they will buy. Make it hard, and you'll be flipping burgers.

Taking the Money

To do the deal and make the sale, you need to be able to take money. In a practical sense, that means you need to be able to accept credit cards—if your only way to receive money is by check, then you will lose 99 percent of your potential business.

Thankfully, it is quite easy to accept money. There are three services in particular that you will probably want to look at:

- PayPal (paypal.com); see Figure 4.2

- Google Checkout (checkout.google.com)

- Amazon Payments (payments.amazon.com)

All of these offer the facility to take charge credit cards on your behalf and to remit the money to you. Naturally, all charge a modest amount for this service, although Google will offset this charge against your AdWords spending (which is discussed later in this chapter). Apart from the charging structure, one key difference is that Google requires the purchaser to sign up for a Google account, and Amazon requires the individual to be an Amazon customer. This is not necessary for PayPal.

If you can't decide which to offer, then offer them all and let your customers use whichever is easiest for them.

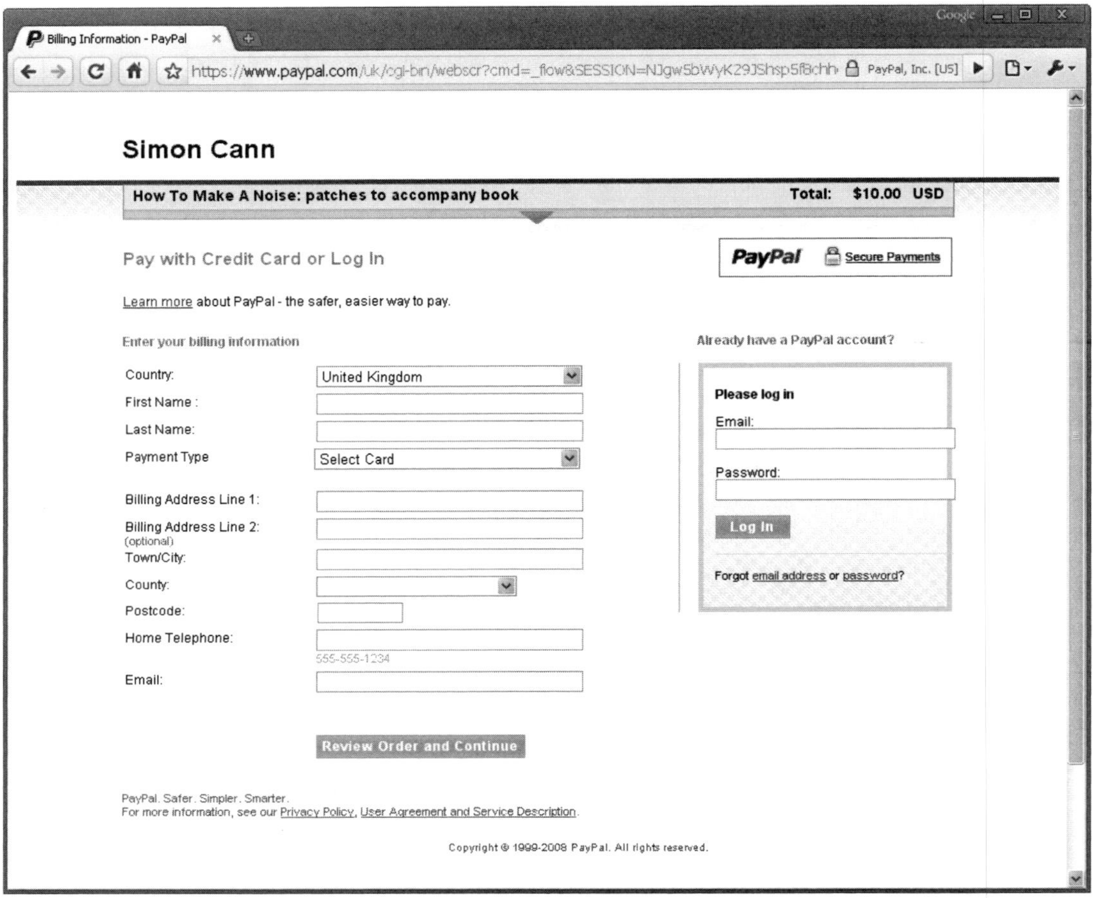

Figure 4.2 PayPal makes it easy to take money on your website.

By the way, when you take money for physical products, remember that there will be postage costs and that these costs will differ depending on where the package has to be sent. You should add the postage costs when charging for any product; otherwise, you may find that instead of making a profit, you suffer a loss on each sale.

Fulfilling the Order

So you've offered your product and made the sale. Now comes the hard part: fulfillment—getting the product to the person who gave you money. Your method of fulfillment will often depend on what you are selling and how you are selling it.

If you are selling a physical product, then you can simply mail the item to the purchaser. However, this approach presents several challenges:

- First, you have to hold the stock—this requires investment to buy the stock in the first place and makes you vulnerable in the event that your stock is damaged.

- Second, you have to physically mail the product to the purchaser. This is a highly labor-intensive process. If you are selling one or two T-shirts a week, it's probably not too much of a problem, but by the time you are sending 15 or 20 packages to people around the world each day, then the job gets quite time-consuming—there is the packaging, checking the order, the receipts, sorting the correct postage, getting the packages to the mail, and so on. This all takes time, and at this level—especially when you have to split the profits—you won't become a millionaire.

However, there are other ways to sell and other forms of product to sell—for instance, you could appoint someone else to sell your merchandise, in which case, your site wouldn't need to sell the products, but you might have purchase links to click the person through from your site. Alternatively, you might not sell your own CDs and DVDs, but instead you could include Amazon Associates links so that people can buy your products from Amazon, and Amazon would then fulfill the order.

If you don't know about Amazon Associates, you should—check it out on your nearest Amazon site (the link is usually at the bottom of the home page). Under the program you still get paid for the sale of your CD in the normal manner; however, Amazon then also pays you commission on all sales that are generated from you referring people to their site.

You may also sell intangible products such as downloads, and as you would expect, you have choices:

- You can set up your own download system, which would probably be expensive and a logistical nightmare.

- You could use a provider such as PayLoadz (payloadz.com) that specializes in making electronic content available. However, with this option, as with your own system, you will only be making your music available to people who come to your website.

- If you want to make your music available in all the major download stores (such as iTunes and Amazon MP3), then you need to use a specialized service such as CD Baby (cdbaby.com) or TuneCore (tunecore.com). If you only want to get into Amazon, then you may use CreateSpace (createspace.com), who can also make your music available through an on-demand CD through Amazon.com if you want. While on-demand cuts your earning per product, it does mean that you don't have stock holding issues and you can scale up your output if needed.

If you are sending traffic to other sites, then you won't have to get your hands dirty handling the finances. This has several advantages:

- You don't have to account for each sale. You don't have to get each sale audited. Instead, you get monthly commission checks (which are likely to be much nicer-sized numbers, assuming you're pushing sufficient business).

- In the case of credit card fraud, it is usually the merchant who loses out. If you're not the merchant, then you won't have the hassle of disputed payments and reversed charges.

There is another advantage to this approach: You don't have to hold stock—that is the job of the merchant. Now clearly, if you have self-pressed a CD, then you will have had to hold that stock. However, once you're in the Amazon (or similar) supply chain, then Amazon will have paid you for their stock, so you will already have the money in the bank. The additional sales you generate keep Amazon (or whoever) ordering more and generate Amazon Associates commission for you.

Mailing List

Your mailing list may be the most valuable asset of your business. It is your direct connection with your source of income—without a future source of income, your business has little future. You should therefore guard your mailing list—in the physical and metaphorical senses—as your most precious asset.

When you build your mailing list, there are several issues you need to consider:

- How are you going to get email addresses?

- How are you going to store the email addresses that people give you?

- How are you going to contact people?

- How are you going to update the contact details?

At this point, I am only looking at the practicalities around email mailing lists—clearly there are similar issues if you are trying to keep any other contact details, such as cell phone numbers to send SMS messages or postal addresses for snail-mail campaigns.

Collecting Email Addresses

You can collect email addresses in many ways. For instance, at a gig people could scribble their email address on a piece of paper and ask to join your mailing list. Alternatively, they could send you an email. The easiest way to add people to your list is to have the functionality built into your website, and of course, there are several routes to this end.

The simplest may be to ask people to send an email (which can be blank) to a specified email address (such as maillist@rockingyourmusicbusiness.com) and then add the address to your list. You might even create a clickable link on your website with a mailto address so that people can more easily send this email. While this has simplicity, it is somewhat clunky, and it has risk. As soon as you publish an email address on a website, it is liable to be harvested by spambots, after which you will start receiving unsolicited email.

To prevent the spambots, instead of displaying your mailing list email address using text, you can convert it to a graphic image. Spambots generally don't know whether an image is a picture of the President of the United States or a graphic representation of your mailing list address.

There are other solutions. My preferred option is to use a web form (see Figure 4.3). This form is then sent to an email address that is hidden from the public; indeed, the destination address has no link with the site itself and so it remains confidential. As this address is only used for mailing list submissions, if it ever receives spam, then all I need to do is close it down and open up a new one. This is two minutes' work for me and will have no effect on the people on my mailing list.

You will also see that in asking people to join, I also show them how they can update their details and, more importantly, remove their name from the mailing list. While these two points are not crucial, anecdotal evidence suggests that people are happier to give their email address when they can see how they can remove their name from that list. You will also see that I have included some words about privacy. While these don't give any enforceable protection, they do help reassure that I intend to use the email addresses I am given in a responsible manner.

Storing and Managing Email Addresses

How you store your email addresses may be greatly influenced by how you intend to send out emails. There are several ways to store email addresses, and depending on how you store them, you may need some manual intervention to transfer the details. You will find any manual processes are tedious and liable to add errors, so I recommend you automate your activities as much as possible.

The really simple way to store emails is to copy all the email addresses you receive into a document or a spreadsheet. This may be simple, but it is not really practical. The other really simple approach is to add the email addresses to the address book in your regular email software (Outlook, Outlook Express, Thunderbird, or similar). Equally, you could use the facility in Google to create an email list.

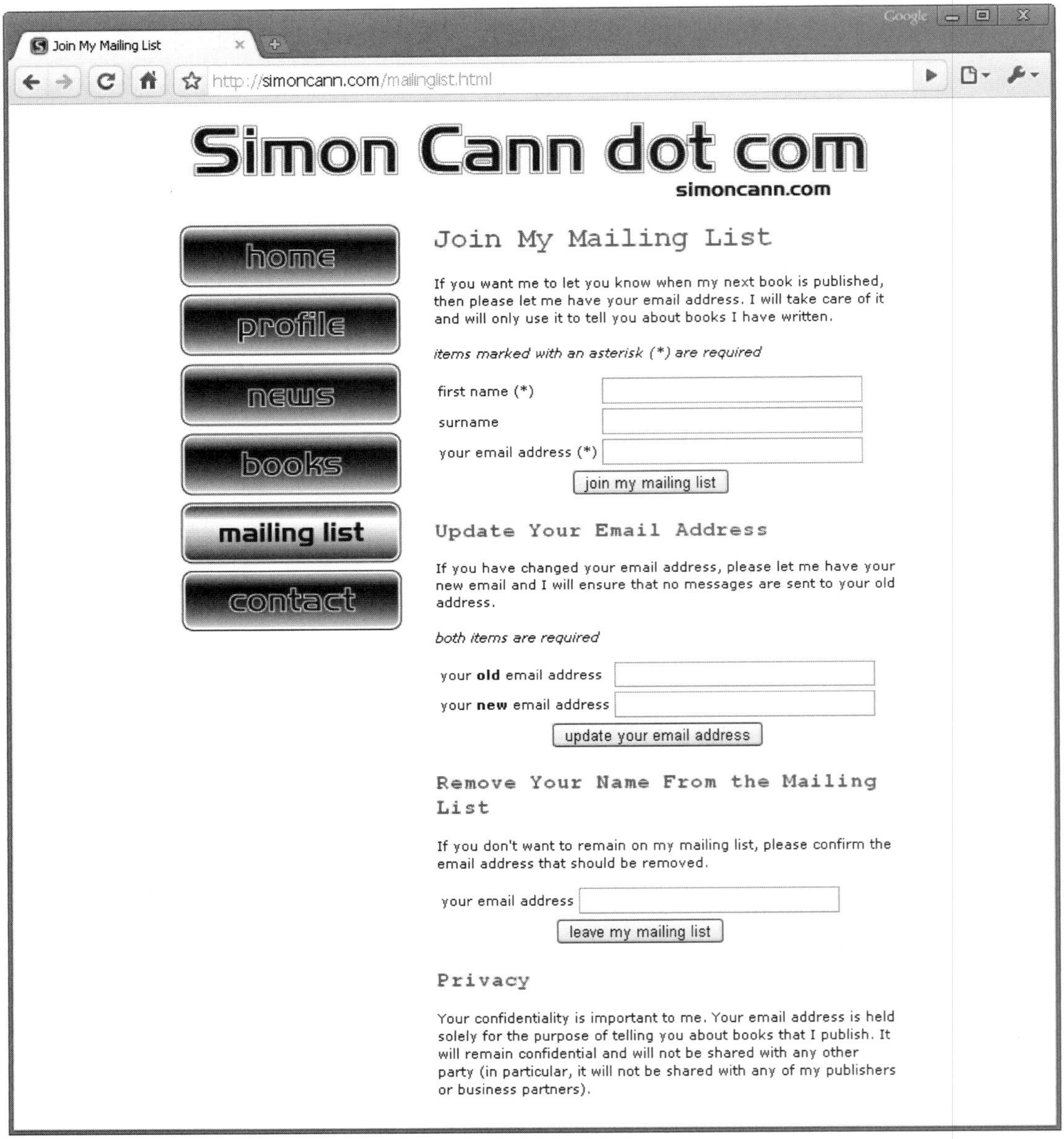

Figure 4.3   A web form to invite people to join a mailing list (in this case, my mailing list).

These options may be feasible if you have a small mailing list, but it will soon become unwieldy if you start dealing with significant numbers. Also, and particularly so for Google, you may have limits placed on the number of emails you can send each day. Many internet service providers impose these limits to prevent spam. Google has limits:

You can send 500 emails (in a period of 24 hours) from a standard Google Mail account or 2,000 from a paid account. For most purposes these limits are fine, but if you want to make a bulk sending, then they are likely to be too small, in which case you either need to split the mailing over several days or find an alternative.

If you're going to store your addresses in a simple manner (such as in an address book), then also take some time to think about how you will deal with:

- Bounces—in other words, emails that bounce back for some reason, whether because of an error, a full inbox, or a closed email address.

- Updates to details. How will people tell you when they have changed their details?

These are all labor-intensive processes if you're managing the mailing list by hand. For instance, if an email bounces, you will often get an email after six hours telling you that there is a problem and that the email system is still trying to process the email. After 24 hours the email system may give up and send you another message. Each message needs to be read and analyzed (or ignored, and you can keep sending out emails to a dead email box and in the process use up your ISP's quota of emails).

Very soon you will find that you need a specialized email provider.

Specialized Solutions

There are many email solutions available. These come in three main forms:

- Desktop software

- Software you can load onto your website

- Third-party service providers

As you would expect, there are advantages and disadvantages to each approach. However, there are several advantages common to all dedicated mail solutions, and these are the reasons you should consider adopting this approach. These reasons include:

- Automatic processing. There are no manual processes—all additions, updates, and deletions can be automatically handled at the individual's request. Equally, you can automatically require "double opt-in," so that when someone subscribes, you ask that person to confirm his or her membership in your mailing list. This helps to reduce errors.

- Facility to set up many mailing lists. Separate lists allows you to target your people and perhaps develop a closer relationship by focusing your email on their interest—for instance, you can make sure you send emails about new merchandise to people who have bought your T-shirts.

- Comprehensive database management tools to allow you to add, remove, and update individuals or groups.

- Bounce and error recording and management. This could mean that if an email bounces (say) three times, someone is then automatically removed from your email mailing list.

- Sending tools that allow you to create and send emails to one or more of your mailing lists.

Desktop Email Management

There are several examples of this sort of software. One of the most robust and fully featured (and the one that I use) is MailList King (xequte.com/maillistking) by Xequte Software (see Figure 4.4). If you speak Mac, then I'm afraid this isn't for you, as it is only available in Windows format; however, there are other choices.

With desktop email management tools, a web form (as was shown in Figure 4.3) can be used to generate a simple email, which is then read by the software. The email will instruct the tool to add, update, or delete the individual and can specify which lists the action should be taken for.

The advantage of desktop email management is that your database is kept on your local computer, meaning that if your website security is compromised, your database is still protected. While there is this level of protection, there is a practical downside to this approach—the tool cannot be accessed except on the computer on which the database is stored. Accordingly, you have a choice:

- You can install the database on a desktop computer that stays at base, and you cannot send emails to your mailing list while you are away from base (which may not be a huge problem and doesn't stop someone from sending an email on your behalf).

- Or, you can install the database on a laptop and carry the laptop with you while you are away from base. This means that you could send mass emails while you are on the road, but your list's security could be compromised if the laptop gets lost.

Whichever option you choose, the system does not need you to access the database in order to work; your website will generate simple emails with the instruction to add, update, or remove people. Somewhere a mailbox will store all of these emails (and

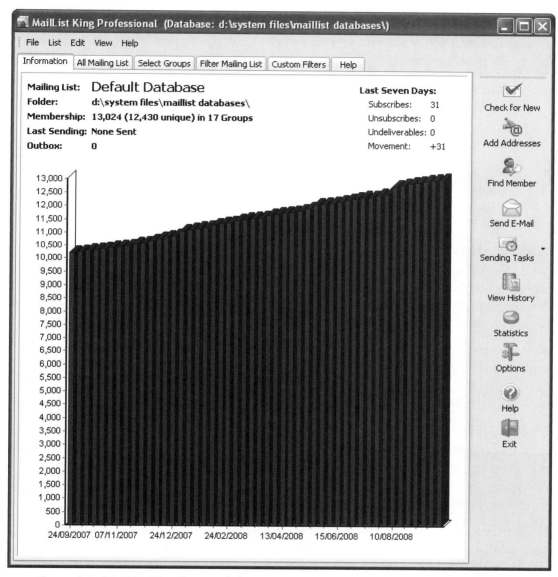

Figure 4.4 MailList King is one of the most comprehensive desktop email solutions. It has many tools—this view shows one of its very basic statistics views.

that could be a Google Mail mailbox) and then when you are ready, you hit the button to access these web forms, and your database is updated. Since the web forms create very simple emails, you would need to receive millions (literally millions) of requests to even dent your storage limit on Google.

A desktop email manager should also handle your email sending. Using MailList King as an example, this tool gives you several ways to send an email. The two that are likely to be of the most use are:

- Sending your mass email through your regular (SMTP) server that you use to send email. This is usually the fastest way to send emails. If your ISP or other SMTP provider places limits on how much mail you can send, then MailList King will throttle the amount of mail.

- Alternatively, instead of throttling, you could use the built-in SMTP server that comes with MailList King. This may not be as fast as using an outside server, but it does ensure that you are not limited to external sending limits.

Web-Based Email Management

Web-based email management employs a tool installed on your website that tightly integrates with your web activities. An example of this sort of software is Dada Mail (dadamailproject.com), which is available for free, although there are options to pay for help with the installation, as there is quite a lot of configuring that can be done.

The configurability also makes these tools very powerful. One example of the flexibility is around how you send an email—you can use your SMTP server to send email (and you can throttle the sending to stay within your host's sending limits), or you can use the tools' own built-in tools, which may not be quite as quick, especially for larger databases.

One advantage over desktop systems is that these offer the facility to access your mailing lists (and therefore send an email to the list members) from anywhere you can access the internet. However, that accessibility means your database is potentially vulnerable to hacking (which could compromise the confidentiality of your list members or lead to their details being deleted).

Rather than explaining all of the features of a web-based email management tool, take a look at Figures 4.5 to 4.11, which illustrate some of the features of Dada Mail.

Third-Party Email Management

There is a third, and more expensive, option to manage your mailing list: third-party email management. These services are more designed for corporate clients who send out frequent emails, perhaps two or three marketing emails a day. As a result, they tend to be comparatively costly if you are holding a large mailing list to which you send emails infrequently.

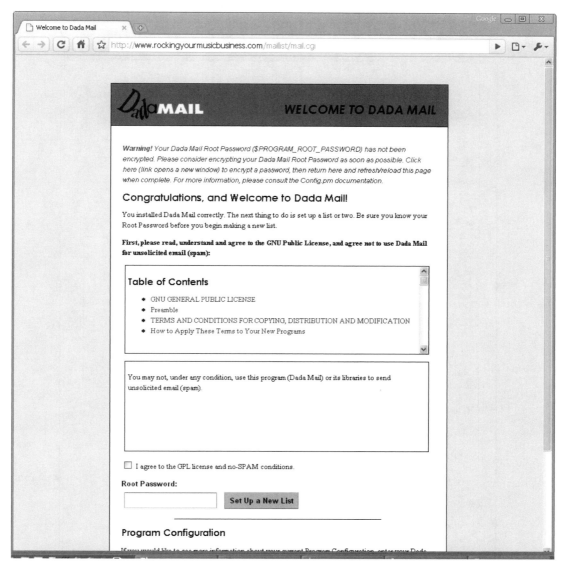

Figure 4.5 After installing Dada Mail, when you first access the tool you come to the welcome message, where you can set the root password.

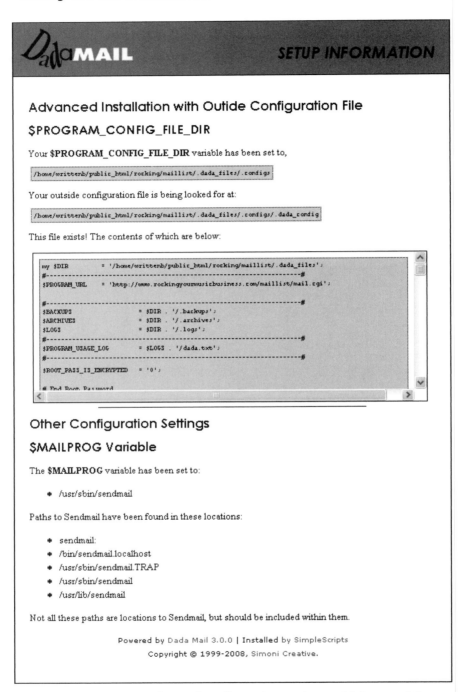

Figure 4.6 There are many advanced configuration options—this is one of the reasons why people get help with their installations.

Figure 4.7   It is a straightforward matter to create a new mailing list.

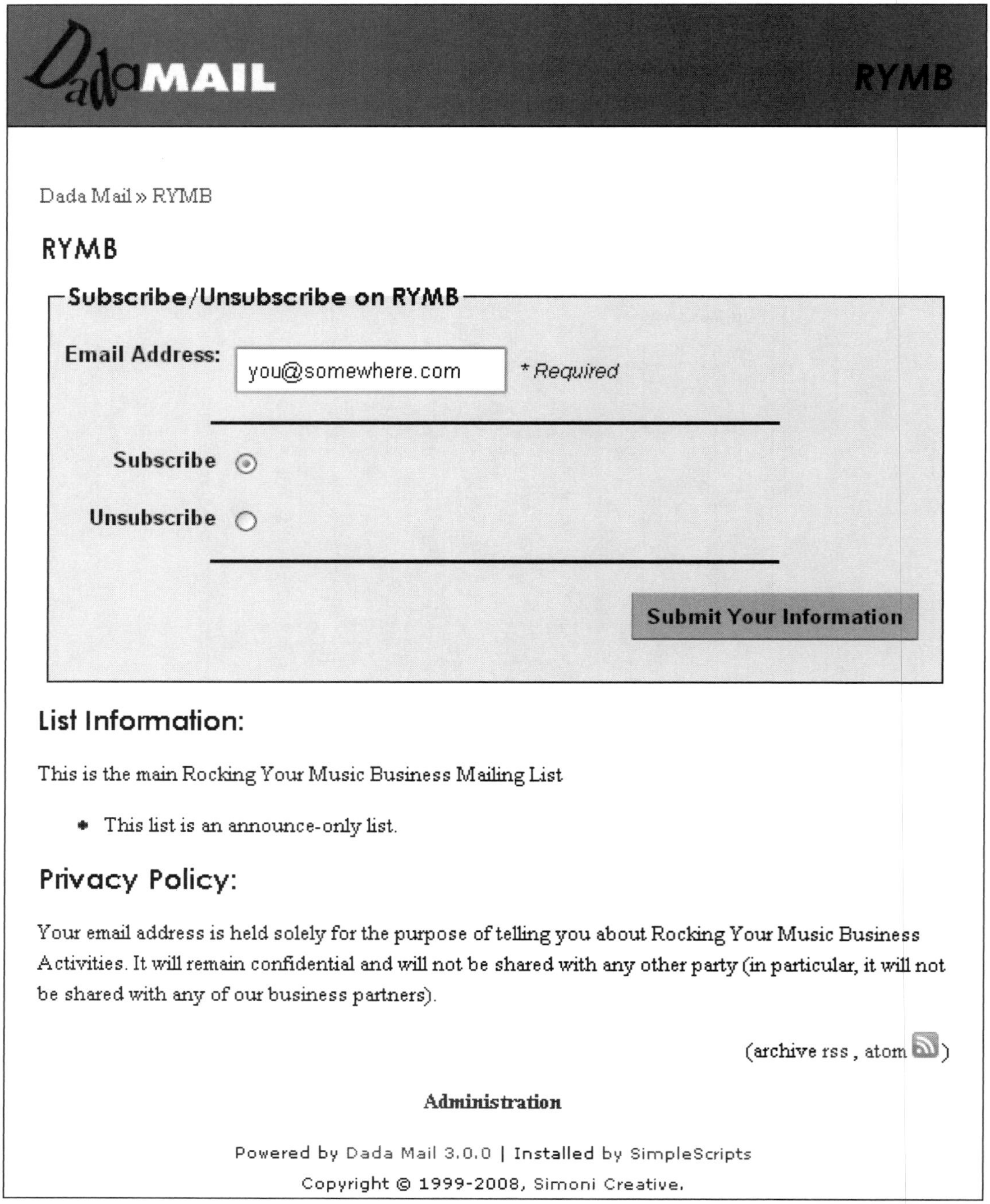

Dada MAIL

RYMB

Dada Mail » RYMB

RYMB

Subscribe/Unsubscribe on RYMB

Email Address: you@somewhere.com   *Required*

Subscribe ◉

Unsubscribe ○

Submit Your Information

List Information:

This is the main Rocking Your Music Business Mailing List

* This list is an announce-only list.

Privacy Policy:

Your email address is held solely for the purpose of telling you about Rocking Your Music Business Activities. It will remain confidential and will not be shared with any other party (in particular, it will not be shared with any of our business partners).

(archive rss , atom)

Administration

Powered by Dada Mail 3.0.0 | Installed by SimpleScripts
Copyright © 1999-2008, Simoni Creative.

Figure 4.8 Dada Mail gives you a simple form to join or leave a mailing list. You will notice that it displays the privacy policy.

Please confirm your mailing list subscription

An email message has been sent to the following address:

you@somewhere.com

to confirm the subscription to the following list:

RYMB

Upon receiving this message, you will need to follow a confirmation URL, located in the message itself.

This confirmation process, known as Closed-Loop Opt-In Confirmation, has been put into place to protect the privacy of the owner of this email address.

If you do not receive this confirmation, make sure that this email address:

maillist@rockingyourmusicbusiness.com

is in your **address book** or **whitelist** .

How to add maillist@rockingyourmusicbusiness.com to your address book/white list

If you still do not receive a confirmation for subscription in the next twenty-four hours or you have any other questions regarding this mailing list, please contact the list owner at:

maillist@rockingyourmusicbusiness.com

Powered by Dada Mail 3.0.0 | Installed by SimpleScripts

Copyright © 1999-2008, Simoni Creative.

Figure 4.9   Once someone has signed up for a mailing list, an email is sent to that person, which includes a clickable link to confirm he or she did intend to join the mailing list.

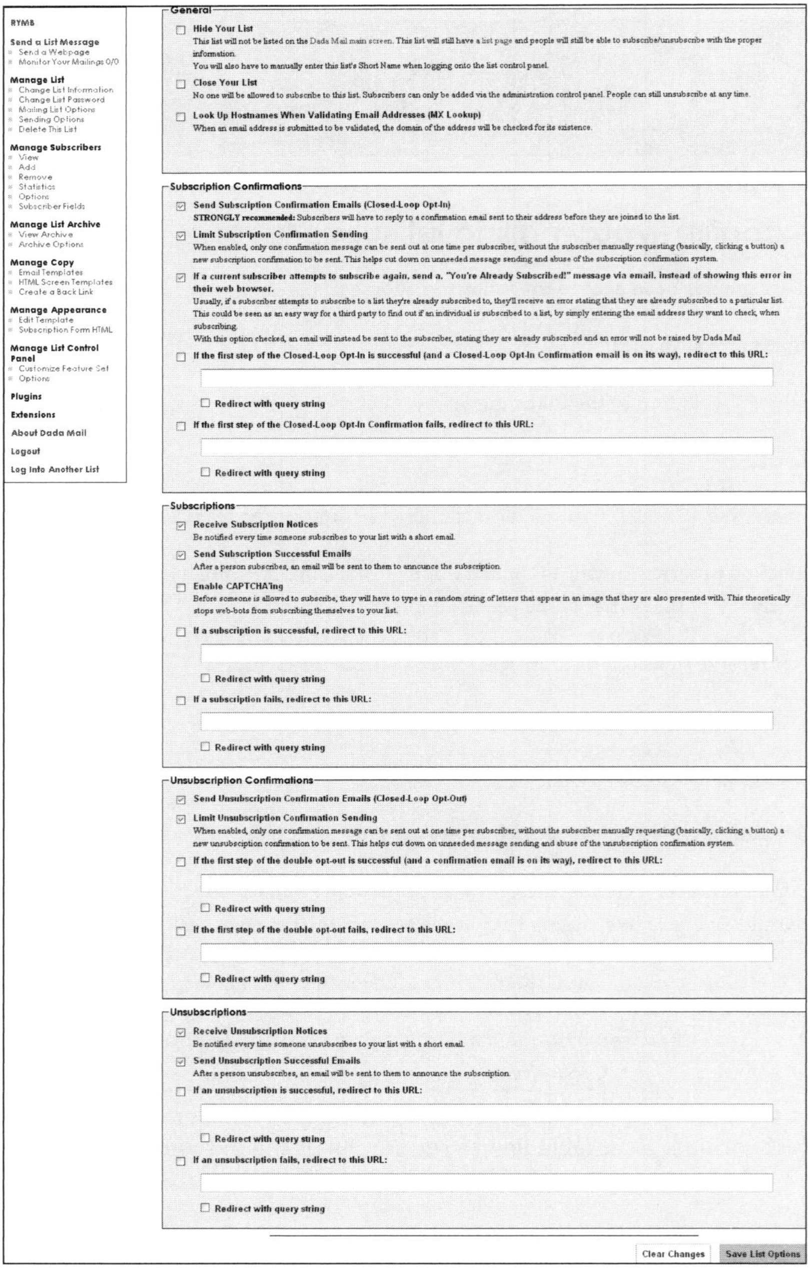

Figure 4.10 Dada Mail offers a huge range of options for how your mailing list is handled. For instance, you can decide whether there should be confirmation emails, and you can decide whether a Captcha challenge is required before someone is allowed to join a mailing list. Captchas are a simple way to check that human beings (rather than machines) are joining your mailing list.

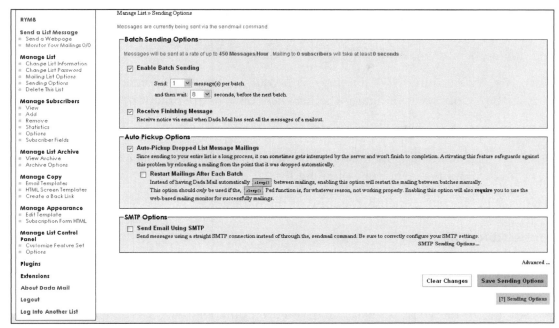

Figure 4.11 Dada Mail offers a wide range of sending options, including the option to send emails through your regular outgoing (SMTP) server, which should give better performance. The advanced options then allow you to throttle the sending so that your servers don't get overloaded.

Who Owns the Mailing List?

Just one point before we move on from the subject of mailing lists...who owns your mailing list? If the band splits, does the list split? Or does the list spend alternate weekends with mommy and daddy? Okay, now I'm being facetious, but this is an important issue and one that I mentioned briefly in Chapter 3.

However, if you want to maintain the mailing list after a band split or reorganization, then there are two issues to consider:

- Data security, in other words protecting each individual mailing list member's details. If the data is passed to anyone, then it should not become publicly available—your messy divorce should not lead to any compromise in the security of people's personal information.

- Using the data in an appropriate manner.

Realistically, in many ways it's pretty tough to figure out who owns the data. However, there is a simple answer: *You* don't own it. People own their own data—they have just lent it to you temporarily so that you can help them know what's happening with your band. They did not give you their data so you could be a pain in the neck and keep spamming them or make the information public.

There are several things you *could* do with your mailing list if someone quits the band/partnership. Only you can figure whether these options are practical, desirable, or legal.

- Retain the data with the original band and do nothing for the departing member.

- Send one email telling members of the mailing list that a member has quit and giving a link to join his or her new mailing list.

- Give the departing member a copy of the data.

Embedded Calendar

A calendar has two purposes:

- First, to tell people who might hire you when you are free.

- Second, to tell your fan base what you are doing and when.

To drive your business forward, you need to ensure that both issues are addressed. This means you need to be disciplined in keeping your calendar up to date, and you need to think about the content from the users' perspective. There shouldn't be any cryptic notes or shorthand—just clear, concise details without ambiguity.

I've already talked about how you can create a calendar feed that people can subscribe to, and of course, this feed should be linkable from your site. However, you can also embed your calendar into your website. This should not be an either/or choice. Your calendar(s) should be:

- Embedded so that people who browse your site can see what you are doing, *and*

- Subscribe-able so your fans can check your feed whenever they want to

When you embed your calendar, you make it available when someone accesses a specific page. (See Figures 4.12 and 4.13 to see how this differs from a conventionally published calendar.) However, unlike a conventional static page, an embedded calendar will automatically display the current month and will be updated to show your current activities (assuming that you have updated your calendar).

The process to embed a calendar is usually very straightforward—your calendar host will give you a piece of HTML code that you drop into your web page, and then you

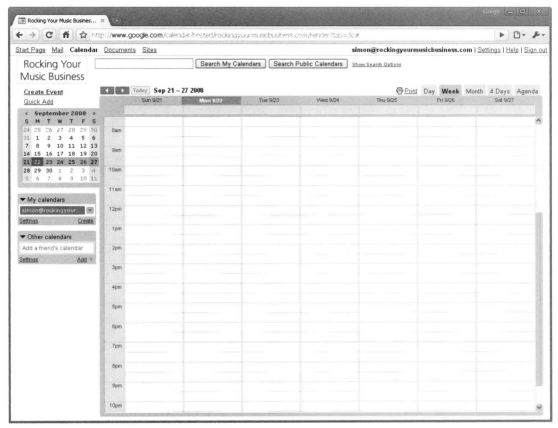

Figure 4.12 A Google calendar. This is how the calendar would look if you accessed it, and it would look very similar if you published the calendar's public address.

will be ready to go. Most hosts will also allow you to customize your calendar (generally in terms of size and color) so that it fits with the look of your site.

Syndicated Feeds

Syndicated feeds is a convoluted way of saying "blog" or "web log," as blogs are often called.

A blog at its most basic is a series of online postings. Often these will be diary-like events, but they can cover a wide range of subjects. For most musicians, the primary use for a blog is to highlight forthcoming events and new products that are available. Because you have your own website (which should include a calendar to tell people

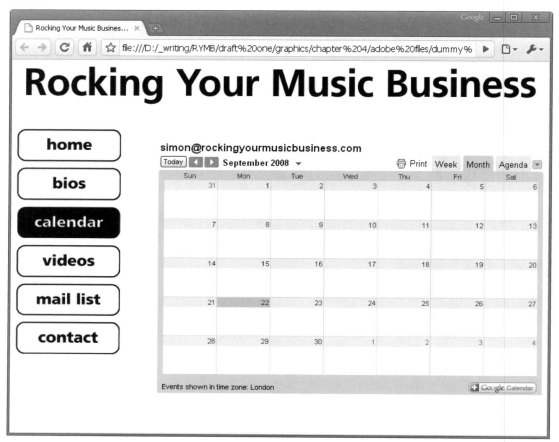

Figure 4.13 The same Google calendar embedded in a website, thereby becoming an integral part of the online business. Google gives you the option to tweak the layout and colors so that the calendar integrates with your site.

about future events), then a blog may not be necessary. However, there is an advantage to these things, and this is why I am talking about syndicated feeds.

A syndicated feed is often identified by its (usually orange) logo; see Figure 4.14 (which will look a bit lacking of color in this black-and-white book). These syndicated feeds are more than simple blogs. While blogs can be produced as simple HTML web pages, these feeds are usually published in RSS (*really simple syndication*) format. This is an XML-compatible feed that can be read through an RSS reader, such as FeedDemon from Newsgator (newsgator.com) or Google Reader.

Figure 4.14 The feed icon, although you are probably used to seeing it smaller and orange.

However, there is another key benefit of syndication—the feed can be picked up and reproduced in other websites. By creating a feed, you are giving people the opportunity to pick up and reproduce your feed. In short, you are giving them a quick and easy way to reproduce any messages you want to publish. You can also (automatically) convert your RSS feed to conventional HTML pages and include them in your website.

If you are particularly technically minded, then you can create your own RSS feed. However, most of us are not technically minded, and for us there is one main option: a blog provider. There are many of these, so let me point you at only two, and you can search for more if you want further choices.

- Blogger (blogger.com, which is part of Google) offers the facility to quickly and easily set up your own blog. This service is free. Figure 4.15 shows a Blogger website.

- TypePad (typepad.com) also allows you to quickly and easily set up a blog. Figure 4.16 shows a TypePad blog. This service is not free, but it does offer a lot more in terms of hand-holding to help you get set up and in terms of additional features. These additional features include:

  - A high degree of control over your layout with lots of add-ons
  - A custom URL (so you don't need to have blogger.com or typepad.com in your feed's URL)
  - Detailed statistics
  - Blogging from your iPhone

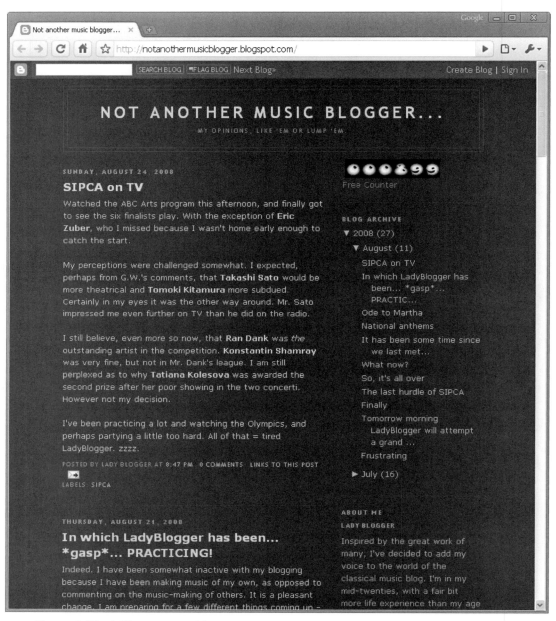

Figure 4.15   A Blogger.com blog.

Figure 4.16   A TypePad blog. Notice the more controlled layout—this is partly due to the author's taste, but is also due to the greater range of features offered by TypePad.

If you are willing to get your hands slightly dirty, then another option is WordPress (wordpress.org). WordPress is an open source software product that allows you to publish a blog on your own website. Figure 4.17 shows a WordPress blog.

Many web hosts offer WordPress as part of their package and have a facility to help install the necessary files with minimum intervention from you. However, you will still

Figure 4.17 A WordPress blog. WordPress offers you extensive layout options, but you may have to work a bit to get the layout you want. For geeks and people who want to get their hands dirty, WordPress may be the answer.

have to do a fair bit of tweaking if you want to integrate WordPress into your existing website.

WordPress is incredibly popular and has many forums to help you get up and running.

Forums

Most web hosts provide the software to set up internet forums on your website. This provides an excellent opportunity for you to interact with your fans and for your fans to talk among each other. However, before you do this, think about the risks:

- Forums without moderators tend to run wild, and moderation requires a lot of time. You don't need to moderate the forum yourself, but you do need to have absolute trust in the people who are undertaking this task. (And yes, I did mean people—if you have a popular forum, then you will need lots of people, not just one person, to help with the moderation.)

- You may not think you have any liability for what happens on your forum— especially if you explicitly state that you are not moderating the forum and you take no responsibility for what goes on. However, does that absolve you of all liabilities? Are you sure that you will not get sued, if only for allowing bad behavior to continue (if it ever happens)? For instance, are you sure you would have no liability if your forum were used to defame, to put forward race hate views, to disseminate a gender-biased perspective, or to breach copyright, just to give a few examples? Even if there is no legal liability, would you like to be associated with a forum where this is going on, and do you think it would be good for your business?

- If you're not there and don't show up to interact with the fans, then what's the point? If you do show up, then you will never be there often enough. Even if you say that you will turn up (say) once a week or every day, someone will find fault.

Forums can be helpful, but they do lead to significant risks if they are not run properly. Before you set one up, consider whether it will drive your business forward.

Contact

One thing you do need is a way for people to contact you.

Clearly this could lead to some challenges—if you have several thousand fans trying to contact you several times a day, then it may be difficult to get through that amount of email. However, when you are trying to build your business, you do need a way for people to be able to get in touch with you. For instance, if there's a problem with your phone or if someone doesn't know how else to contact you but wants to book a gig, then it would be good if they could contact you through your website.

As with your mailing list, you could give out an email address where questions can be sent; however, that would be liable to receive spam, so usually the best solution would be some sort of form that the sender could fill in. Once you have received the email and are sure that this is a person you want to deal with, then you can get in touch using regular email.

Setting Up Your Website

Many ISPs offer free web space. If you are serious about your business, then I suggest you avoid this free offer. There are several reasons for this—these reasons may not apply to all ISP-based web space, but you will often find:

- Unpleasant URLs. Instead of going to myband.com, you will have to have a URL in the form of internetserviceprovider.com/users/files/johnsmith, which doesn't really give the image of a professional business. Even when you get your own URL, you will usually find that you can only point this URL at your free space—when someone bookmarks the page or follows a link, your unpleasant URL will be exposed.

- Slow response time. Free web space is only offered to pull in the suckers—it's not intended to be used for anything other than sharing a few family snaps. As a result, the service will be woefully underpowered. Added to which, when something is free, you can't easily complain about it.

- Lack of features. Again, because it's free, the web space is likely to have a lack of features. So, you won't be able to use your own URL properly, you won't be able to access good statistics, you won't have some really useful email tools, you won't have a file manager, you won't be able to add on additional software (such as WordPress or Dada Mail), and so on.

- One email account. You will often get one email account, and that may well be quite slow and liable to hitches. Again, like the web space, email will not be part of your ISP's core business, so if it is a bit below par for a few days, then most people won't mind. However, if you're running your business, you will notice when the emails stop getting through.

So, if you're not going to use your free ISP space, what do you do? In short, take control and set up your own site. To do this, you need two things:

- Your own URL

- A host to host your site

Getting a URL

A URL is a universal resource locator: It is your web address. So for the BBC, the URL is bbc.co.uk, and if you plug that address into any internet browser, you will be taken to the BBC's website.

You need a URL. Without an address, how will people visit you? However, not only do you need a URL, but it needs to have a certain snappiness and be relevant to your business. Ideally, you will be able to get the band name dot com or similar. However, lots of names are taken, so you may need to use your creativity.

When looking for a new URL, it's always best to steer clear of close matches to avoid confusion—if the dot-com name has gone, don't take the dot-net address: People will get too confused. Equally, single and plural forms can be confusing. Take a look at the names that are similar to yours, and if any are too close, then try something different. Equally, if there are some names that are close to yours that haven't been taken (dot net, country-specific, and so on), think about taking those too and pointing them at your website.

You can't go to a shop and buy a URL; you need to find a registrar. A registrar is a company that is authorized to register domain names. As well as registering, these companies offer a number of other services. Most importantly, they help you set up your DNS record—your domain name servers—the signposts to your website.

Once you have registered your domain, then you have to point it at your host's name servers. The name servers are the signposts once someone has been directed to your host by your registrar's domain name servers. Think of it like a house on a street: The domain name servers point to the street, and the host's name servers point to the specific house.

Typically, your host's name servers will have an address in the form ns1.yourwebhost.com (and usually there will be two of these addresses). All you have to do is plug the address into the appropriate slot in the record for your URL held by your registrar and wait. Usually the changes are instantaneous (or at least within the hour); however, the change may then take 48 to 72 hours to propagate across the internet.

Your host may also give you their server address as a number in the form 223.220.295.131. (Don't follow that—I just made it up.) This is called an IP (or *internet protocol*) address. It is essentially the same as your host's name servers, but a digital representation. I will talk a bit more about IP addresses in the "Dedicated IP Address" section, but for the moment, unless instructed otherwise, you're probably safe to use number or letters—whichever appeals, but then stick with one. However, if you use letters, your website won't cease to work if your host changes their IP address, so you may find this preferable.

Getting your own URL can be a tedious endeavor. It may seem that there are endless obscure questions; however, I cannot recommend strongly enough that you put yourself through this pain so that you directly and "physically" control the URL. If you have control of the URL, then you can make any changes that are needed. If you have a problem, then you can sort it—if your web host goes down, then you can be up and running with a new web host in hours without a problem. Your business won't be out of action for weeks.

If someone else controls the URL—in particular, if the web host who goes down has control—then you could have serious problems. Even if the URL has been registered in your name, you could find yourself having to prove to someone on the other side of the world that you are who you say you are and that you are the registrant of the URL. This could mean that while you are on the road you have to send scanned copies of your passport to prove your identity. It's just not fun having this sort of panic, so take control now.

If you already have a URL, then make sure you have direct control. I don't mean that it is controlled by someone you know—make sure *you* have control.

Once you've got control, make sure that your URL is set to auto-renew so that it will remain registered. If you change your credit card, then update the details with your registrar. You don't want your whole online business to be put on hold because you haven't paid a $10 renewal fee when you are on the Trans-Siberian leg of your world tour!

Finding the Right Host

Once you have a URL, you need a host. The host is where your files are stored and served up to the internet when someone types in your URL or follows a link (perhaps from an internet search engine or another site) to your site.

Spend five minutes on the internet, and you will find a huge range of web hosts. There's always a temptation to go with the cheapest provider, and then you feel your conscience tugging to go with the most expensive on the grounds that they *must* be good for *that* price.

Unfortunately, price doesn't necessarily determine quality of service, although it may give you some indications.

Most hosting tends to be on shared servers. This is where a whole group of websites are lumped together on one site. For many people this is fine. The alternative is dedicated hosting, where the site is placed on its own server.

Shared hosting is usually cheap, but you can have difficulties if someone on your server is running a popular site that slows your server down. Dedicated hosting should make you immune to other websites having an effect on you. However, dedicated hosting tends to cost a lot more (because you have your own server).

The other issue you need to think about is bandwidth. For a music-based site this is a big issue. Bandwidth is the amount of data you are serving up to the web. If you are serving up a page or two of HTML (in other words, tiny text-based files), then you won't have any bandwidth problems. However, if you are serving up audio and video feeds, then you might have problems because these are huge files that constitute a significant transfer of data from your servers to the receiving computer.

This gives you a choice. What you decide may well be driven by cost implications. However, you can take mitigating action. Equally, do remember that most decisions can be reversed—if you are on a shared hosting plan, it can be changed and upgraded. Equally, you can usually trade down from dedicated hosting; however, it's often better to start small and move up as you expand.

Whichever option you take, there is one key requirement that every host customer has: up time. In other words, you want your host to be working whenever anyone tries to access your site. Given that you don't spend all day, every day pinging your site to make sure it is working, this could be a challenge. The site up time is very much the flip side of the coin to bandwidth considerations.

The only option to check your up time—apart from staying awake all the time and clicking on your site—is to use a monitoring service. There are a number of these available, and they offer different levels of service, checking, and reporting. One example of these services is Pingdom (pingdom.com), which offers a range of monitoring and can report to you by SMS message if any problems are encountered.

While it's good to be able to monitor your website, you may not want to make this investment, and in any case, it's preferable to ensure that there are no problems in the first place. Whether you go with shared or dedicated servers, there are a number of options you can consider to keep the load off your servers. If you are going with shared servers, these actions are probably mandatory. While there are other options, let me give you three things to start with—these are all focused on putting the load elsewhere.

Sharing Music: Create a Torrent

As a musician, you are likely to want to share your music. If you don't give people at least a taste of what you do, then you're never going to get them as fans.

In making your music available, you need to acknowledge that—if it is any good—it is likely your music will travel further and wider than you expect and may be redistributed in ways you don't want. Particularly if you get some level of success, you will find people take your music and make it available in ways you hadn't expected and in ways you don't like (for instance, being used as the soundtrack to a dubious YouTube video).

There are two main options you have to react against this:

- Fight it. The best way to fight this action is to never commit anything to a digital medium (such as CD) because anything digital can be easily replicated, and never put anything on the internet because many people will simply see that as an invitation to redistribute your material according to their perception of how copyright laws *should* work. Once you have committed your material to a digital medium and you have found it travelling where you didn't send it, then your likely recourse is to lawyers—such action won't get the results you want, but it will make your lawyer rich.

- Accept it. A far more balanced approach is to accept that your music will find its way to places you hadn't expected. It would be wasteful not to capitalize on this free publicity. The main way that you can capitalize is by driving traffic to your website. When this traffic arrives, you can:

  - Get the contact details of anyone who liked your music, so that you can tell them about your future activities.

  - Sell them stuff. Sell CDs, legal downloads, T-shirts—anything you have to sell.

  - Keep them as fans.

To make sure that traffic is driven to your website, you need to tell people what your web address is. With a video this is simple: You flash the URL on the screen. With audio files this is harder, but not impossible. The "hammer to crack a nut solution" would be to read an advertising message over the introduction of a song—however, that does rely on you having a web address that is moderately easy to say in words. For instance, if your band is called Hot for You, is your web address hotforyou.com, hot4you.com, or hot4U.com? Maybe it's something else altogether.

I'm sure you can see the challenges. The other option is to include something in the audio file's metadata. Metadata is the information about the file that is attached to the files. So for instance, if you have an audio file, there is a data field for the artist's name and a data field for the track name. These fields are what allow you to see the artist, album, track name, and so on when you play a track or search for it. There are other fields—for instance, the Comment field where you can store other data, such as your URL. While this won't guarantee that someone will come to your website, it does give you more of a chance. Of course, you should always make sure that your name is in the artist field (so people can Google you if there is no other way to find you).

If you're happy to send your music into the world, you can put it on your web server with a link to the audio file on a web page. By putting the music on your web server, it will mean that whenever anyone clicks on the link on your web page, your music plays. It will also mean that other people can link to your music too, so you could find your music is played (meaning your bandwidth is hit), but no one is visiting your site, and so you can't sell them anything (which is another reason for ensuring your branding is included in the audio metadata).

To deal with the key issue—bandwidth—there are several choices open to you. One is to set up a torrent such as BitTorrent (bittorrent.com). I talked a bit about setting up a torrent in Chapter 2.

A torrent is a peer-to-peer file sharing protocol that can be used to distribute large amounts of data (audio, video, and any other sort of data). The advantage for you as the initial distributor is that the load on your server is distributed over a large number of servers. When fans then download a file, they do not download it from you, but from a number of peers. This reduces your load (significantly) and also provides excess capacity within the system, making the download more robust.

Another option is to use an external storage service. This is the approach I am suggesting for photos and videos, but it can equally be applied to audio files.

Photos: Flickr/Picasa

Instead of uploading your photos to your website and then taking the bandwidth hit each time they are viewed, your could upload your pictures to Flickr (flickr.com), Picasa (picasa.google.com; see Figure 4.18), or one of the other photo-sharing sites. By embedding the photo, you will be drawing your photo from the external site each time the page on which the photo lives is viewed.

The embedding process is comparatively straightforward. On the page where you want the photo displayed, you include a link. Usually, the link would be to a photo held on your web host server. Instead of referring to that photo, the HTML needs to refer to the URL of the photo on the external photo-sharing site. Put that reference in, upload your page, and view.

There is an alternative approach if you want to reduce the load on your server due to graphics: Reduce the size of your graphics. A reduction in file size usually means a reduction in quality—sometimes the reduction will be noticeable, but often you can make considerable changes before you notice any unwanted results. This approach can be easier than using an external photo-sharing service. However, if you want high-quality graphics and lots of them, then look into external services.

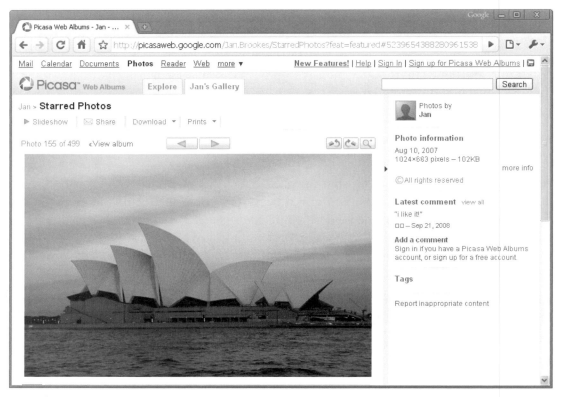

Figure 4.18 Sharing pictures on Picasa—you can also embed photos.

Videos: YouTube

The same principle for embedding photos applies for videos. However, because a video is a much larger file, you are much more likely to want to embed a video. Even better, YouTube make it really easy to embed a video; see Figure 4.19.

YouTube also allows you to customize how your video will look when it is embedded and gives you the option to decide whether to show related videos when your video ends—this might be useful if you want to ensure that viewers aren't distracted by other videos that follow yours and wander off before they have spent money with you.

Once you have chosen the customization options, all you have to is copy the Embed text and drop it into your web page; see Figure 4.20.

Dedicated IP Address

Your registrar's domain servers point to your IP (*internet protocol*) address. With shared hosting, hundreds of websites may have the same IP address. For most websites,

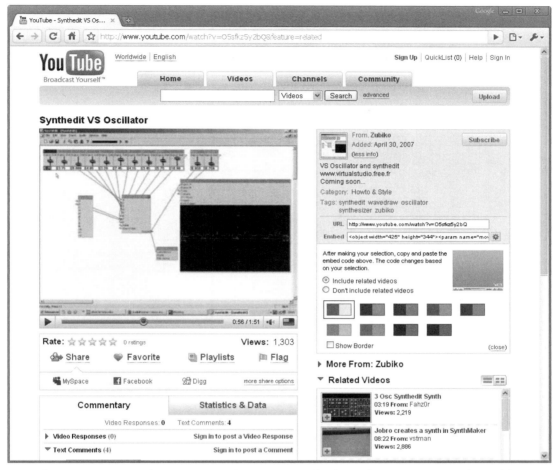

Figure 4.19 YouTube gives you the URL to embed a video into your website (the details are on the right of the screen). You can also customize the look of your embedded video.

this standard practice is not a problem, and indeed, it makes life much easier for the hosting company (and an easy life equates to lower charges, so everyone wins).

I have assumed that you when you take credit card payments, you will use PayPal, Google Checkout, Amazon Payments, or a similar service. This takes away a lot of hard work from you. However, you could set up your own merchant account in order to accept credit card payments directly. If you do this, then you will need an SSL certificate (a secure sockets layer certificate). To use an SSL certificate, you will need a dedicated IP address—in other words, your own IP address.

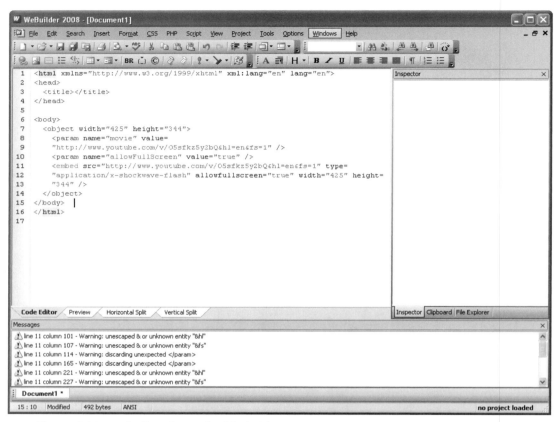

Figure 4.20 Including the embedded video in your HTML.

Another problem with a shared IP address is if someone sharing your IP gets involved with spamming or scamming. This may lead to your IP getting banned or blacklisted. You may not know this has happened until your site disappears from the search engines or your email starts getting blocked by ISPs. In shared hosting the actions of others sharing the same IP can affect your site and cause problems. You may also find your IP address is blocked in other places—for instance, some countries (most notably China) operate a country-wide firewall based on IP addresses. This may mean that if someone sharing your IP is banned, your access to a whole country could be blocked.

A dedicated IP address is usually cheap (perhaps $2 per month). Usually it only takes a quick call or email to your web host to get the dedicated IP set up, and then there will be a brief delay (maybe a few hours) as your host does the necessary work to get you up and running.

As always, this is one of those things you don't need to get set up, but you might want to think about as you grow your business. So, when you choose a web host, make sure you choose one that can offer dedicated IP addresses if the need arises.

Creating Content

When you go to create your website, make it as simple and straightforward as you can. The point is to:

- Draw people in

- Engage them

- Sell them things

- Get their contact details so you can keep in touch

You want to do that in the shortest possible time. You don't need to tell them the whole life story of every band member. You don't need to bore them—this is the entertainment industry, so entertain them.

The things that will sell you as an act are:

- How *you* look

- How *you* sound

To a large extent, how your website looks is irrelevant. It can't look completely amateurish, but you don't need to spend thousands on designers and web programmers. Instead, focus on getting your music and your videos in front of people as quickly as possible. This means no introductory videos that detract from what you're doing and no big buildup—just get to the opening screen and make sure everything a fan wants to see is obvious. This means that on the front page, you should probably include links (note: links, not the content) to:

- Your news

- Your calendar

- Your mailing list signup page

- Your music—perhaps plain audio tracks, but ideally videos

- Your store (even if that only includes links to Amazon)

- Your contact page

When it comes to creating your pages, my personal opinion is that you should edit the raw HTML in a dedicated HTML editor, such as WeBuilder or HTMLPad, both from Blumentals Software (blumentals.net); see Figure 4.21.

Figure 4.21   WeBuilder editing raw HTML.

There are many advantages to editing raw HTML:

- The final pages are much cleaner and don't include unwanted junk. For instance, if you take the HTML output from a leading desktop word processor, it will have huge amounts of junk that you neither need nor want.

- You can see and understand what is happening—this makes fixing problems so much easier. Equally, adding links and so on is usually much faster.

- Faster pages equate to faster loading times—the quicker you get people to hear your music, the sooner they will be fans. Slow them down—especially with video introductions—and you'll lose them.

- Pages produced in HTML are easily searchable by search engines. If you want to be found by Google and the other search engines, HTML is the way to go.

There are other HTML editors. Some web hosts give you an online editor—these are usually quite good, but a bit slow. Alternatively, Google Docs can output fairly clean HTML, and you can also edit the raw code (see Figure 4.22).

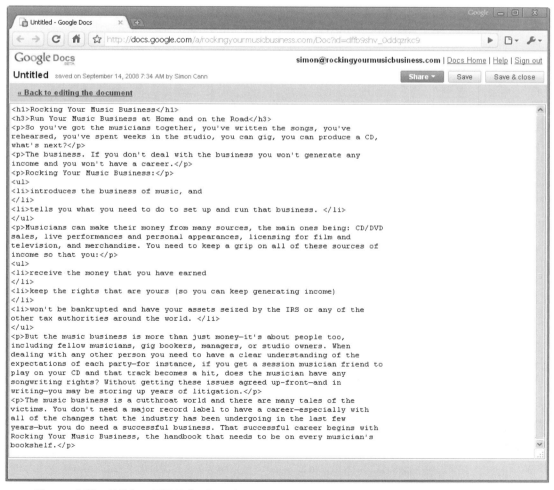

Figure 4.22   Editing HTML in Google Docs.

Bad Habits

Before we end this section, let me caution you against my pet peeves. While these things really annoy me and so to an extent this is purely my personal list of gripes, you will find that they annoy a lot of other people, too. If you can avoid these practices, do—you will thank yourself later when people come to your site.

Speed

Maybe I've got attention deficit disorder, but I can't stand waiting for a website to open. If it takes too long, then I'm off and I won't bother looking.

How long is too long? For me, the longest I will wait is about the time it takes for the BBC news website to open up. (Go to news.bbc.co.uk to check how long that is.) That is one of the most content-rich websites available—why would you take longer than that to load?

Crashes

I can't stand websites that crash or freeze. These problems are almost always caused by dubious plug-ins that are intended to animate the site, which also have the effect of slowing down performance. If you do the raw HTML code thing as I suggest, you should be free from unexpected problems like this.

Requiring Specific Plug-Ins

Some sites require you to have a specific plug-in before you can view their content.

I've got plenty to do in my life and don't need to waste my time, so I don't bother with these plug-ins. Maybe you will find some people who will wait—lots won't, and those will be lost sales.

Site Under Construction and Updating

Websites are not books. Websites are dynamic things that can change. Books are static. If you want to add another page to a website, you can very easily. If I want to add another page to this book when it is in your hand, I can't.

Given that editing websites is so easy, there is no need to add sections where details are still to come. If you don't have any gigs, then don't have a Gigs button with a message saying, "This part of the site is still under construction." It just looks horrible.

If your site is under construction, that's fine—you can launch a site with a limited amount of information. There's no law against that (yet). Indeed, from a practical perspective, you may find it easier to keep adding a page or two at a time to build your site.

You will find that many sites are essentially works in progress that never get finished because the band keeps doing new things or finding new things to sell.

As well as avoiding the Site Under Construction horrors, please keep your site up to date. If you played a gig three months ago, then it doesn't need to be listed. It especially should not be listed if you haven't included your forthcoming gigs.

Also, please make sure that key pieces of information are included on your site. The other day I checked out the site of a guy who I hadn't heard about for a while. The site was strange—it had been updated recently, but something left me unsure, so I went to read about the guy on Wikipedia. It was only when I got there that I found the individual had died earlier this year.

Now, if you die, I won't criticize you for not updating your website. However, if someone is doing some updating, then please ensure they get all of the relevant information up on a timely basis.

Browser Compatibility

There are a lot of browsers available—each will render pages in a slightly different way. With some this may mean that certain features don't behave as they should or as you would expect. This may or may not be a problem. However, as an absolute minimum, I would suggest you check to make sure your pages render as you expect with:

- Microsoft Internet Explorer

- Mozilla Firefox

- Apple Safari

- Google Chrome

Getting onto Google

People will find your websites in three ways:

- They will see it written down.

- They will follow a link from another site.

- They find you from a search engine.

At the time of writing, the most significant search engine is Google. To a great extent, if you are not listed on Google, then you don't exist.

There are two ways you can get listed:

- Sit and wait for Google to find you.

- Submit your site.

Google may find you. If you are linked to by another site, and that site is listed on Google, then when Google's spider crawls that other site, it may follow a link to you. However, it could take a long time before Google finds you, so it's much better to submit your URL to Google.

Submitting your URL is straightforward. Go to google.com/addurl/?continue=/addurl, and you will see a form that looks like Figure 4.23.

Figure 4.23   This is the form to register your site with Google.

As you can see, all you need to do is:

1.   Enter your URL.

2.   Add some comments (but only if you want).

3.   Confirm that you are a human being and not a machine (by decoding a bit of squiggly text).

Google will do the rest.

While Google is the biggest and the most significant search engine, it is not the only one. You will find that many other search engines have a similar submission program. There are services that offer to submit your site to a range of search engines—these may work, but I don't know. My view is that the easiest approach is to select the search engines that matter to you and manually submit to them. If you do that, you know they will come and find you.

Once you have submitted to search engines, then you will hear people talking about SEO: search engine optimization. Personally, I'm skeptical about this as an approach—if Google ever publishes a book on the subject, then I'll believe what I'm reading. My opinion is that if you have HTML pages (which search engines can read) that mention the things that really matter—the band's name, the members' names, and so on—then Google will find you quickly enough.

Social Networking Sites

Repeat after me: Social networking sites do not generate income.

Selling stuff generates income. Social networking sites, such as MySpace, Facebook, and Bebo will help to build your fan base and will help you stay in touch with your fan base, but they will not earn you any money. You may be able to convert your fan base into income, but *on their own*, a bunch of social network "friends" is not income.

I could ramble on for a while about the pros and cons of social networking and the best tools and techniques to deploy, but there is a much easier approach: read *MySpace for Musicians* by Fran Vincent (Thomson Course Technology PTR, 2007). It will tell you everything you need to know.

Equally, blogging (including Twittering; twitter.com) does not drive the business forward in and of itself. Check my comments earlier about blogging for a full explanation. And while we're on the subject . . . yes, you should have your videos on YouTube (and any other video-sharing sites) with your own dedicated channel—especially because this will help take a load off your server and may give you access to a wider audience.

However, having a YouTube channel will not *on its own* generate income: YouTube is only *part* of the online strategy you should be considering.

Advertising

One of the big lures of a deal with a major record label is the advertising budget.

I must confess that I am pretty skeptical about advertising for many reasons. In the context of music, my main concerns are:

- I don't believe it works. Okay, that is a bit harsh—some advertising can connect. However, a lot of advertising is just wasted money.

- The advertising is effectively paid for by the musicians. At this point you will probably be jumping up and down and saying, "But the money comes from the label." While the label may pay, where do they get their money?

Although I might be skeptical, that does not mean you should dismiss advertising out of hand. Indeed, there are some things I think you should try, but these are very dependent on the nature of your business.

Local Advertising/Specifically Targeted Advertising

Let's say you're a band and you specialize in playing at weddings.

Up and down every country, people are getting married every day, and there will often be a bash afterward where there is a band. Generally people go into marriage with the intention that it will be their only marriage—alternatively, they go in with the notion that it will be their last. However often a bride or groom gets married, they don't tend to create much repeat business for the band that plays at their wedding. For instance, they are unlikely to book you to play at their anniversary party or their next wedding. . . .

This means that the band that is hired to play at a wedding will be doing its first piece of work for their client on the big night. To get a first piece of work, you have to sell your services, and before you can do this, the prospective client needs to be aware of you.

Wedding bands are often recommended by couples who have had a good experience and guests who have enjoyed a band. For this reason, smart businesspeople in these sorts of bands will have lots of promotional material readily available when they are playing at a wedding.

However, many wedding bands get hired without recommendation, so how do these bands come to the attention of the happy couple? Well, two of the most obvious ways are through advertising and through encouraging related businesses to refer business.

When it comes to advertising, then the obvious place to advertise is in a wedding magazine. If you're a prospective bride, then your life will be all-consumed with all things wedding, so it is unlikely you would be looking for a band in your regular subscription to *Welder's Monthly*. However, you may well see an ad in *Walking Down the Aisle Monthly* and decide to check out the band's website or ask for their demo package (which may include a marketing brochure with some nice words and photos of the band in action, a CD/DVD, and some recommendations).

If you're looking for other people to recommend you, then the obvious places would be wedding related: cake decorators, caterers, wedding dress shops, and so on. Perhaps you could leave some of your promotional literature and ask them to give it out.

Now, I'm not suggesting that this is the way to fame and fortune in the wedding-band industry, but I hope you see the essential point that I am driving at: Any advertising and marketing activity has to be highly focused, and even then it will generate a very low hit rate.

But let's say you're not a wedding band—instead, you're a Metallica tribute band, and you've got a gig coming up. Is it worth advertising?

In this situation, I could see groups of people who may be interested in this sort of a gig (beyond your family and friends):

- Metallica fans who want to hear Metallica songs played live

- Regular gig-goers looking for a good gig

I will deal with Metallica fans later in this chapter, but how do we attract the attention of regular gig-goers? Unfortunately, the options are limited:

- If the venue has a mailing list, then it will probably have sent an email to everyone on that list already.

- Clearly, there will be some advertising around the venue. However, on its own this may not necessarily pull in many people.

- My best guess for potential audience members would be teenage males, so you would need to figure out where these guys are. I'm not suggesting that different ages or females wouldn't be interested—I'm simply trying to guess where you would get the most return. In this context, you may find groups of these young gentlemen in college—perhaps you could put up some posters around nearby colleges. Perhaps there are one or two radio stations that are focused on this market, and you could either get yourself interviewed on the station or run a few ads (as long as you can keep the price down).

Online Advertising

I will deal with Google, Yahoo!, and other search engine advertising in a moment. There are many other online advertising options: One of the most obvious options is to buy advertising space on a site that may be related to your music business. So looking at our two earlier examples:

- If you're a wedding band, then you might want to consider advertising on a website that features wedding-related issues.

- If you're a Metallica tribute band, then you might think about advertising on a Metallica fan forum or a thrash metal discussion forum.

While these smaller-scale advertising outlets may cost less, you should carefully consider the effectiveness of your advertising. For instance, if you're that wedding band and you are based in New York City, will it be cost effective to pay for advertisements that people in Europe, Africa, and Asia will see?

Only you can decide how effective online advertising could be. If you are going down this route, then I would suggest you limit your exposure until you are certain that it works.

Wider/National Advertising

If money is no object, then you could pretty much keep spending money on ads until the end of time. As with online advertisements, with other forms of advertisements you need to consider whether print, TV, and radio advertisements will:

- Bring you business

- Bring you the business you want

Or will the advertising be wasted because it reaches people outside of the geography in which you are working? If you're launching a CD that you want to sell globally, then a broad advertising campaign may be appropriate, but if you're that wedding band or that Metallica tribute band, then you may find better ways to spend your money.

Wider advertising may work, and it may not. However, before you put your hand in your pocket, take some time to think about how much money you are prepared to risk. Not only that, but how much money are you prepared to spend in order to achieve an unquantifiable return?

Search Engine Advertising

Search engine advertising is potentially a hugely powerful tool. It's also a potentially expensive one. A $10 daily budget may seem modest, but after a year that translates to nearly $3,700, which is a reasonable amount to spend if you generate enough income to pay for the advertising and make a profit. If you don't, then $3,700 is a lot of money to spend for nothing.

If you don't know about search engine advertising, these are the ads that come up next to your search results when you query a search engine (see Figure 4.24). These aren't random ads; they are advertisements where the advertiser is specifically targeting the words you searched.

So, for instance, if you take a look at Figure 4.24, you will see what happened when I Googled the word "elephant." The first sponsored link is for elephant.co.uk, the website for Elephant Car Insurance (which is an insurance company in the U.K.—unfortunately, it's not a joke). This link shows up in a box above the main search results. Then on the right side of the screen, there are other sponsored links to:

- The World Wildlife Fund (logical...they help support elephants)

- Another U.K. insurance company—this is a smart bit of marketing and one I will discuss shortly

- Save the Elephant (again, logical)

- A car insurance comparison site

- A program to foster elephants

All of these links have come up on the very first page of search results because someone has paid for them. It has nothing to do with the search engine's search algorithm or search engine optimization of any sort—it is pure advertising.

The leading proponent of this form of advertising is, of course, Google, and I will talk more about what they do in a moment. However, there are other search engines that use this approach, too—for instance, Microsoft's Live Search, Yahoo!, Ask, and AOL all have sponsored links.

Google calls the program by which you can sponsor links AdWords, and I will look at some of the things it can do for you in the next section. Just to make sure we're clear on terms, I should also mention their AdSense program.

AdSense is the arrangement where Google pays you to carry their ad. If you have a website and you include ads from Google, you can get paid. Think of it like a

Figure 4.24   Ads showing in a Google search—the ads are at the top of the search and to the right of the main results. (They are indicated by the Sponsored Links note.)

magazine: AdWords is for the advertisers who want to promote their product, and AdSense is for the publisher of the magazine who gets paid to carry the ad.

Google AdWords

Google AdWords isn't the only sponsored search engine program, but it is one of the most popular, and since Google is the most popular search engine at the moment, it is the one that gives you the widest potential reach. Also, many other search engines (for instance, Ask and AOL) also carry Google AdWords ads. Not only that, but the program that allows a lot of flexibility that isn't available in other programs—for instance, you can target ads by geography (even down to ZIP codes).

To run an AdWords program, you need to do a number of things:

1. Set up a Google AdWords account. This is free (of course—they want to hook you in to start spending money). To set up an account, you go to adwords.google.com.

2. Write your ad.

3. Identify the keywords you want to use.

4. Set a daily budget.

5. Set a maximum cost per click.

6. Run the campaign.

Let's look at these steps in a bit more detail.

Write Your Ad

Take a look at Google, and you will see that ads take a pretty standard form. There's a reason for this—Google restricts how much text you can use. You are allowed a heading, two lines, and a URL tag.

Before we get to the text, don't overlook that URL. Google allows a specific URL to be used for each ad—that allows you to set up a customized "landing page" (in other words, a page that will display when an ad is clicked). This means you could have different ads clicking through to different pages. So take our wedding band: Perhaps they also play corporate functions, and when they do their set is less romantic and more funky. With AdWords they could run separate campaigns targeted at different markets and linking to different areas of their website, but to the areas that have relevance to what the potential customer is looking for.

You have to make your ad short and sweet—this is not the time for soaring prose and sweeping descriptions. Just look how much space you have (these are the limits—you don't have to use all the space):

- Heading line: 25 characters.

- Line 1: 35 characters.

- Line 2: 35 characters.

- URL line: 35 characters—however, this is the maximum length of the displayed URL. The URL you click through to can be up to 1,024 characters.

As you can see, space is pretty tight. In total (excluding the URL) you get 95 characters. To give you a comparison, this paragraph contains 157 characters.

Given the limitations of space and that all ads are essentially experiments, Google lets you try things out. You are not limited to one ad—you could have several different ads running (at no extra cost) and then choose the one that works best.

Identify the Keywords

Once you have your ad text, you need to choose your keywords. This is where you need to (1) pay attention, and (2) be clever (or devious), as this allows you to precisely target your audience.

Your keywords are the search terms against which your ad will be shown. So in the example I showed earlier, the keyword that those six ads had bid for was elephant. Clearly, you don't want the word elephant, but the choice of term will be significant, and you should take your time over it.

So, taking our wedding band, there's an obvious term for them to use: wedding band. However, that could lead to an ambiguity. What happens when people are looking for rings—in other words, wedding bands for their fingers? How do you differentiate?

With any text-based search, you're going to have to accept that where a word can be interpreted in two ways, there will be confusion. The only answer to avoid ambiguity is to use unambiguous terms, so "wedding entertainer" may be a better term. However, you could spend a long time finding a clear and immediately understood term, but then end up with something that has no relevance or a term on which no one would ever search.

Clearly, there is a balance to be struck, and you need to find a term that has sufficient relevance to the service you offer. This is also where the advertisement's wording is important: With those 95 characters, you allow your potential client to be able to immediately understand whether you are a show band or a jeweler.

On the flip side, the ambiguity could always work for you. You could find that someone who is looking for jewelry for their wedding stumbles across you by accident. Don't dismiss this option—there are worse ways to get business. However, I wouldn't build a business on this strategy alone.

That's the wedding band sorted, but what about our Metallica tribute band? There's a really sensible keyword here, isn't there? "Metallica."

At the time of writing, Metallica is about to release a new album and will be touring in support of that album. However, when I Google Metallica, there are only two paid advertisements: one for an internet radio station and one for a ticket agency (selling tickets for Metallica gigs).

I don't know how many Metallica fans there are out there—I would guess a lot—and I don't know how many want to see a Metallica tribute band—I would guess some—and I don't know how many of those people would be close to where this mythical tribute band might be playing—perhaps a few—but I hope you see that this gives you one way to connect directly with people who have an interest in Metallica.

This principle also applies to many other bands. If you think your music would appeal to, say, Deep Purple fans, then why not use Deep Purple as a keyword? When I last searched on "Deep Purple," there were no Google AdWords.

The great thing about keywords is that you don't have to limit yourself to one word or one phrase. You can choose a whole range, so you could have "Metallica," "thrash metal," and "heavy metal" as separate search terms all associated with a single ad. You will also find that Google provides you with a range of tools to be able to generate keywords and make estimates as to their effectiveness.

Set a Daily Budget

When you have your ad and your keywords set, you then need to set your budget. The budget is the maximum daily amount that you are prepared to spend. With AdWords you only get charged when someone clicks on your ad—you don't get charged when your ad is served up. Your ad will keep getting served up until there have been sufficient clicks to exhaust your budget, and once your budget is exhausted, then your ad will not be shown again on that day.

While you set a daily budget, Google will apply this rate over each billing period, so if you set a budget of $1 per day and there are 31 days in the billing period, then your maximum cost will be $31. If on any one day your budget is not met, then the excess may be used on another day.

Especially if you have a low budget, you could reach your budget quite quickly, which may mean your ad only shows for a short period of time. Google does have tools to help you spread your budget so that ads are displayed over a longer period or at specific times. However, these tools won't get you more hits if your budget is low.

Also, there is a trend to make ads less enticing, which is, of course, highly counterintuitive. However, this practice does have benefits:

- The ads are served up more times and so will show over a longer period.

- There are fewer clicks, but those that come through may be from more dedicated individuals, not just people clicking anything that looks vaguely interesting.

As with all things internet-related, this is a nice idea, but it is hard to prove that it actually works in practice.

The daily budget is the tool to control costs. If you are interested in trying out AdWords or one of the other search engine advertising programs, then the budget will allow you to test the system while containing your costs. You could, quite literally, set the budget at $1 per day and then only run the ad for seven days, thereby limiting your spending to $8. (I've added the additional dollar in case you don't switch off the ad before the end of the day.) This doesn't give you a zero-cost trial, but it does allow you to test your ad's effectiveness very cheaply and to tweak the ads until they work, after which you can start ramping things up.

Set a Maximum Cost-Per-Click

The daily budget on its own doesn't achieve much—and it is rather an intangible notion when not put into context. To understand the context, you need to get a grip on the Maximum Cost-Per-Click (often called CPC) by Google.

The Maximum Cost-Per-Click is the maximum amount you are willing to pay when someone clicks on one of your ads. This is a figure that you and you alone set. There is a minimum that varies by country. For the U.S. it is 1 cent; for the U.K. it is 1 pence.

When somebody clicks on your ad, the maximum that you will pay is the figure set by your Maximum Cost-Per-Click. The amount you pay will be subtracted from your daily budget, and your ad will keep getting served up until you have received sufficient clicks to exhaust your budget.

If you get no clicks, then your ad will keep getting served up, and you will not spend anything.

As you can see, there is a link between the Cost-Per-Click and your daily budget. If you set your budget at $1 per day and your Maximum Cost-Per-Click at $1, then you could blow your budget with one click. However, if you set your budget at $100 and the Maximum Cost-Per-Click at 10 cents, then you may get 1,000 (or more) clicks.

Once your budget is spent, that's it for the day: Your ad will not be shown again until the next day's budget is available.

Now, the obvious answer is to set a low Maximum Cost-Per-Click in reference to your daily budget—that way your ad will keep getting served up. That is true; however, there is another issue to consider: the position of your ad.

The position of your ad in the list of featured ads is not a matter of chance. Those at the top pay more, and those at the bottom pay less. Worse still, if you choose a particularly popular keyword (or phrase), then your ad may not even show on the first page. Some Google AdWords listings go on for several pages.

There are two ways to come higher up on a listing:

- Bid higher.

- Choose less popular keywords (which, as noted earlier, is likely to move you further away from your target audience). However, there are some words/phrases (such as Metallica or Deep Purple) where you could be on the front page for a minimum-level bid.

As you set your Maximum Cost-Per-Click at a higher level, your ad will show higher in the list. In essence, the way the system works is:

- Each business that wants to use an AdWords ad will set its own budget and Maximum Cost-Per-Click.

- When someone searches on the keyword, Google will look to everyone who has budgeted for that keyword and will then charge according to what has been bid. The highest bidder will get the priority position, and the following ads will be ordered according to the amount they have been charged. You don't necessarily get charged the maximum amount of your bid, but you will get charged more if you bid more.

If you want to be top of the list, then obviously you have to bid more than anyone else. Google provides tools so you can estimate where you will come; however, the best way to see where you fall is to run the ad and put in your keyword. If you do this, don't click on your ad, because you will be charged!

Google does not disclose what other people have bid, and they do not notify you about activity on your keyword or give you the chance to outbid other people. Equally, due to the nature of budgets and the length of campaigns, you may find yourself at the top of the list one day, on the third page the next, and at number five the day after.

As your ad is clicked on, you may find that most of your daily budget has been spent, meaning that you only have a few cents left to spend—your bids will be tailored accordingly so you can keep spending to the very end. There is another facility so that your ad will not be shown below a certain minimum position if you want to avoid coming out on page four.

You can use this positioning feature to ensure your bid really counts. You can do this by bidding low and then specifying that you want a top-five position (for instance). At the start of the day, when budgets are full, you will always be outbid. However, as these higher bidding competitors run out of budget, there is room for some of the smaller guys who will then still have budget left. Now clearly, this doesn't guarantee that the other bidders' budgets will run out, but it is one way to ensure that you have a chance if there is an opening (and you don't look cheap by turning up on page five).

The other point to note about this strategy is that the higher up you are, the more you get clicked (because people tend to start at the top of the list and work down). People at the top also tend to get clicked irrespective of whether they are absolutely relevant. The net effect is that you will usually burn through your budget faster as you get higher on the list.

Run the Campaign

Once you have got all the pieces in place, then you can run the campaign.

You can stop at any time, and equally you can revise the campaign at any time—this stuff is all done online, so you don't need to ask permission. You just need to hook up to the internet and do it.

Because it's so flexible, you can change any detail and keep changing details until you get it right. So you can set a higher or lower Maximum Cost-Per-Click and a higher or lower daily budget. Equally, you can change the text or set several different wordings to rotate. When you start to look at your click-through rates and your website hit rates, you will be able to assess how effective the campaign has been. If you really want to dig into the statistics, you can sign up for Google Analytics, which will help you get a really firm grasp on what is happening on your site. You can find out more about Analytics at google.com/analytics.

Fine-Tuning Your Targeting

Google also provide some great ways to really target your ad. For instance:

- You can target your geography, either by limiting the country or by specifying a more precise location. This means you can target your ad to people searching in the locality you specify. Going back to the wedding band, this may be really useful if they don't want gigs more than 100 miles away from base—for this sort of band, there would be little point in advertising globally. You can also target by language— if (like most English speakers) you only speak English, then you can exclude your ad from non–English speaking sites (however, then you may not reach people using non-English sites who speak English).

- You can set your ad to show at certain times of the day with Google's scheduling feature. If, for instance, your ad is primarily aimed at the teenage market in a specific country, you may want to exclude the period when most people in this market are likely to be at school or asleep. By scheduling your ad in this way, you will be likely to get more appropriate clicks.

- Google will spread your ad to a certain extent so that you won't blow your budget in the first five minutes of operation. However, you can also choose to have your ads spaced over a longer timeframe so that you have the opportunity to reach people at different times.

There are also lots of other features Google offers that can help make your ad more effective. Take a look and see for yourself.

Audio Ads

So do you want to get on radio, too? After all, you're all about the music, aren't you?

Well, Google can come to the rescue there, too, with their Audio Ads service. At the moment, it only covers U.S. radio, but that's a pretty big market. The system is rather like search engine ads (but without the keywords). You select your geographic regions and your target demographics, and then you bid (having set a maximum budget). You can read more at google.com/adwords/audioads.

If you're just starting out, then this option almost certainly won't be for you (unless, of course, you like giving your money away). However, if you are an established band with some proven success, this may be an option for you. Also, you might want to consider collaborative advertisements. Say your band only has $1,000 to put into advertising—perhaps there might be another four or five bands in your area that have a similar budget. Alternatively, you might be able to find some other friends on MySpace who have a modest budget. If your collective could raise in the region of $5,000 to $10,000, then you could have enough money to fund a real campaign.

Clearly, a short radio commercial wouldn't give you much opportunity to promote five (or maybe more) bands (and equally you're unlikely to have five bands from the same region that are all looking to release a CD at the same time). However, you could all work together on a collaborative project—for instance, if the bands were to collaborate and play a gig together, this gig would be worth advertising. The gig would then also:

- Create a real event where you could all bring your fan bases together, thereby creating a critical mass.

- Allow each band to cross-fertilize their audience. Potentially, if there are five bands with roughly the same size audience, then you will have the ability to reach a new audience that is four times the size of your current audience.

- Create something that is worth publicizing.

Although it may seem odd to create something just so you can take advantage of an avenue of publicity—and you should ensure that you only collaborate to further your music career and not to further your interest in advertising options—this is one of the opportunities to place yourself on the same level as a band signed to a reasonable-sized record label. Not only that, but by collaborating you will be helping to create and foster a scene, and a scene will always be more vibrant and will draw more publicity than a single act.

One word of caution: These radio ads cost a lot more than search engine ads, even if you are able to bid for the lowest prices. Please don't spend any money you don't have, and please do not spend money until you have some way to assess the return on your investment in a moderately empirical manner.

Go Do It Now

Now this may sound like a slightly glib comment, but it is intended as a serious point.

If you are interested in search engine advertising, or you are enthused by its possibilities, and you have read the caution in the next section, then the best way to *really* understand what AdWords does and what it could do to help propel your business forward is to try it out. When you try it out, you will find those "a-ha" and "so that's how it works" moments. You'll also find yourself saying, "Wow, this is really cool! I can do this too . . . ," which is pretty compelling.

I would encourage you to set up an account and take a look around, even if you don't run a campaign immediately. This will give you an idea about all the choices and tweaks that are there. Then try a limited campaign—perhaps limit your spending to $10. (If you can't afford to lose $10, you really are in the wrong business!)

The key with any test (once you have ensured that you will not spend lots of money) is to be able to measure what the AdWords service does for you in terms of increased traffic.

A Warning about Advertising

There are many compelling reasons to think about advertising—any sort of advertising. As you can see, Google in particular seems to offer some real possibilities at a good price. However, before you spend a cent, let me give you some warnings.

- Advertising costs can mount very quickly. Daily rates can be very deceptive—they look small, but when you're out of the office for weeks at a time and not paying attention, you can find that a few bucks a day has become hundreds of bucks, and if you let the program run for months, you can spend thousands very easily.

- Advertising will not bring you sales. Never. Advertising will generate interest—that interest is of use to you only if you can convert it into sales. While an improved hit rate on your site will massage your ego, it won't put a cent in the bank. Also, you will never be able to scientifically prove that one person has found you and spent money with you based on hearing an ad, therefore you will not be able to draw up a formula that says $X spent on advertising will *definitely* generate $Y income.

As long as you understand that advertising is a very dull tool that will only generate interest for a high cost, you will be fine. Just remember, what you really want is word of mouth, and that is free!

5 Accounts, Records, and All Those Pieces of Paper You Need to Keep

We can talk, can't we? I mean, we've been through a lot together—well, four chapters at least—so now we can share something that we'll keep between ourselves, right? Is that a deal?

Okay. Then let me tell you a secret: Accounts are not the most interesting topic in this book (see Figure 5.1). They're not even the most interesting topic in this chapter. However, they are vitally important, so you need to pay attention, but I'll make this chapter as brief as humanly possible. How does that sound?

Before we go any further, can I add two notes of caution?

- First, as I always mention, there are different accounting requirements in each jurisdiction, and this book makes no attempt to explain the specific requirement of any jurisdiction.

- Second, accounting is a vast and complicated subject. As with any vast and complicated subject, there are many opinions about the right and wrong.

As always, the best approach (and usually the one mandated by law) is to seek the opinion of an appropriately qualified accountant within the jurisdiction in which you are operating.

Why Do We Care about Accounts and Records?

Ultimately, accounts and records are important for one reason: money. The accounts are the tool that we use to make sure the money is right—if we don't have the accounts, then how can we be sure about the money?

Take a look at the main purposes of the accounts and see whether you think anything can be ignored.

- Accounts record how much money has been received and from whom it was received. As part of the process of checking how much money you have received, your accountant

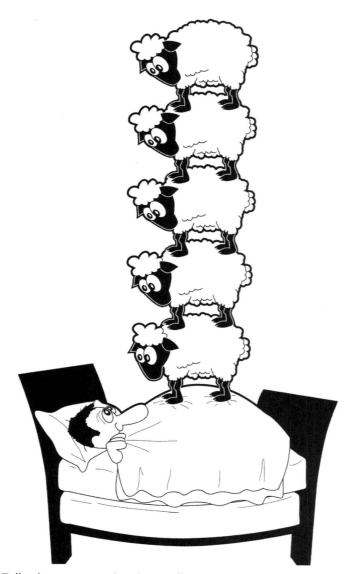

Figure 5.1 Talk about accounting is usually enough to send most people to sleep.
© Robert Balazik I Dreamstime.com

can (and should) check how much you should have received, so your accounts may be the first time you find that an amount due to you has not been received.

■ Accounts record how much money you have paid out and to whom the money was paid. From this information you can confirm that the correct amounts were paid out and check whether any amounts were paid that were not intended. Equally, you may find that critical payments—for instance, your tax bill or your insurance premiums—were not paid.

- Having checked the income and the outgoing payments, you will be able to determine what is left. If you have less left than you should have, that may mean you have been defrauded—in other words, you have been ripped off. Very often accounts are the first place where people find they have a problem.

- Having determined what is left at the end of the year (and assuming you haven't been defrauded), you will then be able to determine:
  - Any tax liabilities. While you may not want to do this, the alternative—not paying your taxes—has very unpleasant consequences (which include losing assets as part of a bankruptcy action and going to jail in certain circumstances).
  - Each member's share of any profit (or loss).
  - The value of the business, and therefore, each member's interest in the business.

There is another reason for keeping accounts and records (which is partly linked to the tax issue): In most jurisdictions there is a legal requirement placed on businesses to keep records, and usually those records need to be retained for at least six years. You need to keep records for several reasons—first, tax, and second, particularly if you have limited liability for your business, it is often a requirement that records are made publicly available.

I will talk some more about tax in the next chapter.

Paper Trail, Audits, and Records

Quite often it's difficult to get a grasp on what "accounts" means (see Figure 5.2). Let's look in a bit more detail at the elements that go into your accounts.

Paper Trail and Records

The world that we live in thrives on bits of paper. Occasionally, these bits of paper don't make it from electronic into real form, but there is still a strong impetus to create a hard copy of the document.

Whenever you go into a store and buy something, you will always be given a piece of paper. This isn't simply a certificate to mark the store's gratitude that you gave them

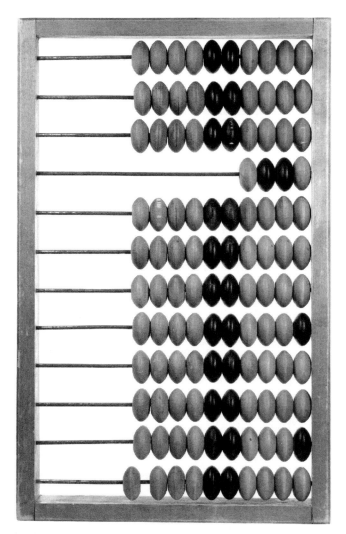

Figure 5.2   Is this how you see accounts? © Yuris I Dreamstime.com

some money: Each receipt will detail the transaction. Specifically, the receipt will usu-ally tell you:

- Where you shopped—the store name (including the full legal name of the business), the address of the store with its phone number, and the registered office of the business.

- When you shopped—the date of the transaction (and usually the time).

- What you bought—the product names and the quantities of each product.

- How you paid—usually with an indicator of which credit card you used.

You may get other details—for instance, who served you or which pump the gas came from—but as you can see, there is a lot of detail in there.

And what do we usually do with these bits of paper (see Figure 5.3)?

Figure 5.3   The stack of receipts we all collect when we've been buying things.

Well, if you're anything like me (and Figure 5.3), then your receipts will pile up at home. However, many receipts get used to pass on phone numbers, wrap up used chewing gum, or stop a table from wobbling. If you're one of the people who does this sort of thing, please stop now!

All receipts related to your business should be guarded. They are records of your business and prove that you have made business-related expenditures.

Each receipt that you receive should be looked after with the same care that you would use to guard any other document that belongs to your business. If you got a contract with a major record label, you would keep that document in a safe place, wouldn't you? Your approach to receipts (and any other financial documents) should be the same.

All receipts you receive should be kept in a safe, secure place, so that your accountant, bookkeeper, or whoever draws up your accounts can draw up accurate records. Also, if any receipt you receive does not contain sufficient information for your bookkeeper to be able to draw up the accounts, then additional information should be recorded. For instance, you might have a receipt for an airline ticket—simply being a receipt does not confirm that it is a document that relates to your business. However, if there is a note (either written on the receipt or written on a separate sheet of paper attached to the receipt) confirming that the receipt relates to tickets for the guitarist and the drummer flying to the recording studio, then the bookkeeper will be able to confirm that the correct details are recorded.

As well as receiving receipts, you are likely to issue them, too. For instance, whenever you sell any item, then you should give the purchaser a receipt. Again, you should keep a copy of all the receipts that you issue in a safe place so that your bookkeeper can draw up your accounts.

From time to time you may receive (and you may issue) invoices. Invoices are a notification of a requirement to pay—they are not evidence of payment. You should retain a copy of any invoices and then ensure that you get a receipt for each invoice you have paid.

Let me summarize this section: Keep a copy of all your records in a safe place and pass them to someone sensible to draw up your accounts. If you can't afford to hire someone to draw up your accounts (and if you can't find a practical way to hire a remote worker to undertake this task), then you're going to have to do it yourself. Unfortunately, as soon as you have any level of success, it will take a long time because there will be a lot of pieces of paper to reconcile.

Audits

The next section looks at drawing up accounts. Before we get there, let me briefly mention audits.

An audit is a review—usually undertaken by a qualified accountant and usually undertaken on at least an annual basis—to confirm that the books are in order. Audits seem to upset people a lot, and if you've got a bookkeeper, then any audit will probably upset him or her. However, audits are vital, so learn to deal with upset people.

As the business owner, the auditor should report directly to you. He or she will not report to your bookkeeper, your accountant, your manager, or anyone else within your organization. As a first step, the auditor will check that your books are in order. Auditors do this by ensuring that the accounts agree with your records. If you have not kept your records, then this will be a challenge for the auditor.

However, the auditor will usually go beyond checking your recordkeeping and draft accounts to look at how your whole business is run and will often express an opinion about the business's compliance with appropriate laws and regulations.

If the auditor cannot form a satisfactory view about the operation of your business, then he or she will qualify the accounts. If an auditor qualifies the accounts, this doesn't mean the auditor is disagreeing with you (necessarily). Most often it means that he or she believes something is wrong with the accounts. This could include fraud or it could include poor recordkeeping by you. Ignore these warning signs at your peril—if you are serious about your business, then take these warnings seriously and sort out any problems.

Drawing Up Accounts

Once you've got all your bits of paper together, you would hope that the accounts are straightforward. After all, it's only a case of adding and subtracting all the elements!

Unfortunately, it's not quite that simple. Let me elaborate a bit.

Elements in Accounts

Before we do anything, we need to understand the main elements within accounts. Broadly speaking, each item will be classified into one of five broad groups:

- Assets
- Liabilities
- Equity
- Revenue
- Expenses

Let's look at those in turn. Once we've looked at the elements, then we can look at the accounts you can draw up.

Assets

In very broad terms, assets are things that you own, and so would include cash, bank holdings, instruments and other equipment, and so on.

Liabilities

Your liabilities are your debts—money that you owe to other people. So if you have an invoice you have yet to settle, that is a liability of the business.

Equity

When a business is established, owners will usually put in some initial funding. This is the initial equity of the business (sometimes called *shareholder equity*).

In really crude terms (and I mean *really* crude—I apologize to any accountants who may be wincing): Equity = Assets − Liabilities. If the value of the liabilities exceeds the assets, then there is negative equity which—depending on the legal structure of the business—may mean that the asset holders have an additional personal liability.

Revenue

Your revenue is the income that you generate from your business activities, so for instance, if you play a gig, sell a CD, or sell a T-shirt and you get paid, that income is your revenue.

It is important to be able to distinguish between assets and revenue. Revenue is the income that you receive, while assets are everything you own. Once you have received your revenue, then it will be part of your assets. There are several reasons for making this distinction:

- You will usually be taxed on your revenue, and not your assets (although if your assets generate income—for instance, cash at the bank may generate interest—then that will be income, too).

- You need to understand how much money flows from each activity. If you buy 100 T-shirts for $1,000 and sell them for $750, then you will have made a loss. If you cannot identify the income that has arisen from any activity, because your assets and revenue are confused, then you will not be able to identify losses.

Expenses

Your expenses are your costs and anything else that means you have less money. In short, whenever you spend money, it is an expense that must be accounted for. However, when you spend money, you often get something in return, which will then be an asset of the business—for instance, if you buy a guitar, then you have the expense, but you have the asset (that should go on your balance sheet).

However, there are three types of expenses:

- Operational expenses
- Capital expenditure
- Financing expenditure

These are discussed in the following sections.

Operational Expenses

Operational expenses are your main day-to-day costs. So for instance, your staff costs, gas for the van, and rent for your rehearsal space would all be operational expenses. Generally, these expenses are not made to buy something that will remain as an asset for a long time (so for instance, the gas you buy will be used as you drive around).

When you account for operational expenses, you record the full expense when it is incurred.

Capital Expenditure

Capital expenses are costs that are incurred buying assets for the business. For instance, if you buy gear, a van, or a studio, those would all be capital expenses. With capital expenses you usually expect to then have an asset with a value and which could be sold.

A key difference between operational expenses and capital expenses is how they are accounted for. Operational expenses are accounted for in the year in which they are incurred, but capital expenses are often spread over a number of years—the notion is to spread the expense over the period the asset has value for the business.

Financing Expenditure

Financing expenses are the costs that are incurred in raising money for your business. Typically, this would be the expense incurred on paying the interest on any loans or other sorts of business finance that you may need to put in place.

Cash Flow

Your cash flow records income and expenditure—quite literally, the cash that flows into and out of the business. Your cash flow statements are very much like your bank account statements, showing income and expenditure (see Table 5.1), and allow you to easily see your earnings and expenditure over a set period.

Table 5.1 A Cash Flow Example

Income	Expenditure
Income from gig	$100
Gas to get to gig	$30
Sound-system hire	$20
Total earnings	$50

Cash flow summaries aren't only used for simple cash flows—for instance, they can be used to record the changes in values and notional payments. As mentioned earlier, when a capital expenditure is incurred, while the payment may be made immediately, the cost recorded in the accounts can be spread over several years. Equally, the value of the asset will (usually) decline over time, and this decline in value (called *amortization* in accounting-speak) will be recorded, too.

Balance Sheet

Cash flows only show money in and money out—they don't give any idea about the value of a business. By contrast, a balance sheet (which is sometimes called a *statement of financial position*) will summarize the value of a business.

A balance sheet is the document that brings all of the accounting elements together and is usually comprised of three elements:

- Assets
- Liabilities
- Equity

The important piece for your business is equity. The equity of a business is the value of a business. Although that may often seem like a rather abstract concept, it shouldn't—it is the financial equivalent of your hard work and success. The owners of most growing businesses keep their money in their business—they usually do this for two reasons:

- They don't know how much they can take out because on a day-to-day basis, they don't know what the business is worth nor what bills and other debts need to be paid.
- They want to leave the money in the business to grow the business.

As a result of keeping money within the business, the business owners will often have comparatively low earnings for a few years. However, this is balanced out by having a very valuable business.

Valuing Assets

When it comes time to work out the balance sheet, one of the hardest tasks is to value the assets. The reason for this is that many assets do not have a value that can be readily assessed. For instance, take the example of a car. If you go to a showroom, then the dealer will quote you a price—after a bit of haggling you might agree to a figure.

If you buy the car and drive it home but then decide you don't like it and go back to the dealer, the dealer won't usually buy it back for the price you paid. If you go back to the dealer 12 months later, the price of the car may have fallen even further (typically between 33 percent and 50 percent).

Now, we all understand this notion of depreciation, but the idea of "value" is much harder. What is anything really worth—what is the car worth in this example, and what someone will pay for it? And what is something worth when it is intangible? For instance, what are your copyrights worth? This is a tough issue: Your copyrights could generate income for up to 70 years after your death, so they clearly have a value, but you don't know how much income they could generate.

However, there are probably more pressing issues to think about than what your songwriting royalties might be 50 years after your death—for instance, debts. If anyone owes you money, then that will be an asset of the business that could be included on your balance sheet. Simplistically, you could include that debt as an asset.

You could, but with any debt there is a possibility that the debtor will not be able to pay you. If any business that owes you money goes into administration/bankruptcy/chapter 11 protection, then you may receive either less than is owed to you or nothing. For this reason it is worth chasing all money that is owed to you (or, more to the point, paying someone else to stay on top of this).

Of course, another time when you need to think about valuations is when you are splitting a business. This will typically happen when someone is leaving and wants to take his or her share of the business. Often the breakdown in business relationships follows a breakdown in the personal relationship, so things can get pretty rancorous.

At this stage, people often want to keep everything for themselves and destroy anything they can't have. If you want to do that, go ahead. It certainly makes the valuation easier—if you destroy the business, it is worth nothing, and sharing nothing around is easy. Everyone gets nothing!

So if you are splitting the business, please take a sensible and pragmatic approach. Also, look to the effect that the departure will have on your future income. If you are a duo and are splitting, then it's likely that half of the business won't be worth 50 percent of its value. In reality, people will come to see the duo, not the two individuals—therefore, on your own, each member of the duo is likely to earn less than half of what he or she would have earned with the duo. You can keep arguing with both parties, trying to extract 50 percent of the pre-split value, but you will never reach a satisfactory solution in these circumstances.

Accounting Tools

This chapter has only scratched the surface of accounting—there really is a lot more to think about, but let me leave this chapter with a final thought about the mechanics of drawing up accounts.

When it comes to your accounts, you can use a spreadsheet; however, you will probably find the limitations of your spreadsheet fairly quickly. For instance, you won't be able to reconcile various amounts—as an example, you won't know whether an invoice on one sheet is related to a payment on another sheet.

The best way to stay on top of your accounts is to use a specialized accounting program. Before you purchase any software, it will be worth having a word with your accountant. If you can choose software that is compatible with his or her software, you will often find that you can share information more easily, and the cost of your annual audit will drop.

6 Government and Officialdom: You Ain't Gonna Fight the Law

Y ou can run . . . but it's too much of a rock and roll cliché to get caught. So many "rich" musicians have been bankrupted by not paying attention to their legal obligations (in particular, by not paying taxes).

But since those joyous times when musicians could earn a fortune and then be bank-rupted by the tax authorities, the weight of legislation has increased. Not only is there more legislation covering every aspect of our lives, but we all live international lives now. No longer do musicians make a living without travelling outside of their state—with the internet, we are all global performers generating income from around the planet, and for those who do play live, the opportunities and the infrastructure to play gigs around the world offer options that could not be conceived of 20 years ago.

Rather than try to explain every piece of legislation in every state, country, and separate jurisdiction, this chapter sets out the broad principles behind most of the common entertainment-related legislation in the developed world. Before you get too global, you might want to have your lawyers give you some advice!

Tax

There's an old cliché that the only certainties in life are death and taxes. While this cliché is probably correct, it fails to highlight the nature of tax and its pervasiveness. Governments need to raise tax so that they can spend money and, since the cost of everything always seems to be going up, tax always seems to be going up. Clearly, any government that increases tax rates is going to lose favor quite quickly, so govern-ments are finding different ways to levy taxes, especially in ways that don't upset the people who vote for them. There are now four main ways tax is raised:

- Personal taxes—these are taxes that are imposed on individuals. Usually people will be taxed on their earnings and their investments.

- Corporate taxes, which are levied on companies.

- Capital taxes, which are levied when individuals or corporations sell an asset at a profit.

- Sales taxes (or value-added taxes), which are levied on most things we buy (with whatever income we have left after income tax has been levied).

Let's look at these in a bit more detail.

Personal Taxes

Most governments tax their citizens directly. More than that, they require employers to collect the tax and then remit it to the government without the employees having sight of that chunk of their money. The rate of tax that you will pay is determined by your domicile (essentially, where you live) and the amount you earn.

Typically, you can earn a certain amount before you get taxed. For instance, currently in the U.K., you can earn just over £6,000 before you start to pay tax. When you cross that threshold, you then pay 20 percent of your earnings (in excess of the threshold) as income tax. In the U.K., when your salary then hits £40,000, tax is payable at the higher rate of 40 percent—in other words, 40 percent of your earnings over £40,000 goes straight to the government.

There are special allowances in certain circumstances, but as a general principle, something just under half of your earnings for a U.K. citizen can be taken in tax. While the tax systems around the world all vary—in particular, the rate of tax that is levied varies—most apply a similar principle: You get a basic allowance and then start paying tax, and when you reach a certain level, the rate of tax goes up.

Most income tax systems work only to tax their own citizens, so visiting foreigners do not get taxed. This is quite reasonable—you may well feel aggrieved if you came to London for a holiday and were given a tax bill that you had to settle before you were allowed to leave. You would probably be doubly upset because you would probably also be getting taxed at home. However, in some jurisdictions visiting entertainers and visiting sportsmen do get taxed.

Social Charges (Including National Insurance Contributions)

While not a tax, it is worth mentioning social charges at this point, if for no other reason than they feel like taxes and they are often collected by a jurisdiction's tax collection agency.

Many countries have social charges that are levied on individuals in addition to their tax, and there is often a parallel charge on employers. These charges are intended to fund social welfare programs to a greater or lesser extent.

Unfortunately, there's very little I can say about these payments that is positive. You're just going to have to comply and pay the money (and deduct it from your employees if you are required to do so).

Corporate Taxes

Corporations also get taxed. However, unlike individuals, corporations are allowed to set expenses against their tax liability. Let me give you an example—take a corporation that earns $1 million and has expenses of $900,000. If the corporation tax is paid at the rate of 25%, the earnings would split as shown in Table 6.1.

Unfortunately, it's not always that simple—often companies are not allowed to set certain expenses against their profits. If we take the example used earlier, but assume that only $700,000 was due for tax relief, look at what happens in Table 6.2.

Table 6.1 A Basic Corporation Tax Calculation

	Amount
Earnings	$1,000,000
Expenses	$900,000
Pre-tax profit	$100,000
Tax	$25,000 (25% of $100,000)
After-tax profit	$75,000 ($100,000 − $25,000)

Table 6.2 A Corporation Tax Calculation Taking Account of Expenses

	Amount
Earnings	$1,000,000
Expenses	$900,000
Tax-allowable expenses	$700,000
Taxable earnings	$300,000 ($1,000,000 − $700,000)
Tax	$75,000 (25% of $300,000)
After-tax profit	$25,000 ($1,000,000 − $900,000 − $75,000)

As you can see, by only allowing certain expenses, the tax burden can become dispro-portionate. One of the expenses that is typically not allowed is entertainment. This means that if you charge your partying to a company, the tax man will effectively charge the company tax on your partying.

However, it doesn't end there. Not only do the tax authorities want to tax your party-ing, they want to tax companies when they give money to their shareholders.

There are two ways to get money out of a company:

- Salary
- Dividends

If you take any of the company's earnings as salary—rather than leaving that money in the company—the salary you receive will then be taxed as regular income. The upside is that salary will be an expense for the company and so will reduce the company's tax bill (although personal taxes are usually higher than corporate taxes, and will also incur social costs).

The other way to take money out of the company is as dividends. In essence, dividends are a share of the profit paid to all shareholders (so if you hold fewer shares, you will get a lower proportion of any dividend). Dividends are taxable as income for the recipient, and furthermore, in most regimes, that tax (at least at the basic rate) is levied at source (in other words, the company is legally required to deduct tax before it pays a dividend). However, dividends are often exempt from social charges.

There is a third way to generate income from a company: Sell your shares. While you will gain the income from selling the shares, you will subsequently own less of the com-pany (meaning your income will be less in the future), and you will be liable for capital taxes (which are discussed in the next section) on the sale.

Capital Taxes

Capital taxes (sometimes called *capital gains taxes*) are levied when you sell an asset for a higher price than you paid for it.

So for example, say you bought a modest recording studio for $250,000 and then sold it for $1 million. That would create a capital gain of $750,000. If the capital gains tax were 20% (which is a figure I have plucked out of the air—you will need to check the rate in your home jurisdiction and maybe the jurisdiction in which you dispose of the asset)—that would lead to a bill of $150,000 (20% of $750,000) for selling the studio.

Naturally—this being tax—there are more wrinkles, and life isn't always that simple. For instance, some jurisdictions allow gains to be offset against other losses. So in this example, if you sold one recording studio and bought another, then you might be able to "roll over" your gain, and you would pay tax when you sell that second asset. Equally, in some jurisdictions your asset can appreciate in value (perhaps in line with consumer prices) without incurring any capital gains liability.

Sales Tax

Sales tax (often called *value-added tax* or *VAT*, and sometimes referred to as *indirect taxation*) is legally required to be added to the cost of products and services in many jurisdictions. The requirement to add sales tax/VAT is determined by the jurisdiction into which the product is sold, so if you are an American citizen selling T-shirts in France, then you will be required to comply with French laws for VAT (and it's not just France—VAT applies throughout the whole European Union).

Sales over the internet is one area where the law is still struggling to keep up with current practice, so there will be oddities and misunderstanding (as well as difficulties with enforcement). Generally, sales tax will be charged on domestic sales (if the country levies sales tax), but will not be charged on exports (or exports outside of the EU for any European Union resident). However, if sales tax has not been added, then import duty will be paid in the importing country (at a rate that is broadly equivalent to the sales tax if the product were purchased in the importing country). But don't take my word for it—legislation is always changing.

There is usually a threshold below which businesses do not need to charge VAT; currently in the U.K. that level is £67,000. That means a band could earn £67,000 before it would need to register for VAT. This is significant since VAT in the U.K. is currently payable at the rate of 17.5%. Let me put that in context—if you are selling a CD for £10 before registration, then after registering for VAT you would have to sell the CD for £11.75 in order to keep the same income.

However, VAT is not all doom and gloom. It's pretty dire, but there is one upside. As a business, your suppliers will charge you VAT, so if you go into a studio, to take one example, you would be charged VAT. When you are registered for VAT, you can offset the VAT you are charged and the VAT you are required to charge. For this reason, some people register for VAT even when they are below the VAT threshold so they can save costs. If this seems strange to you—and it is—then it is worth remembering that VAT (as with most sales taxes) is intended to be a tax on consumers, not on businesses. However, the way that VAT is charged and collected means that businesses are required to work as the government's collection agency.

Tax Avoidance and Tax Evasion

A quick word about tax avoidance and tax evasion—there is a difference between the two: whether you go to jail.

Tax avoidance is a legal behavior by which you arrange your affairs in the most favorable manner so as to minimize your taxable liability. This is a good thing! Provided you hire a smart accountant, he or she should be able to find many ways to keep your tax bill to the absolute minimum.

Tax evasion, on the other hand, is illegal. Evasion occurs when you willingly misrepresent your income—in essence, you lie in order to reduce your tax bill. Again, a good tax adviser will tell you when your behavior is likely to fall foul of the authorities.

Of course, there are always behaviors that are hard to categorize. For instance, bartering is quite a problematic option for tax authorities. For a start, it is much harder to find a paper trail and to audit a barter transaction. Beyond that, it becomes increasingly difficult to ascribe a value to bartered items. Please don't shy away from unconventional approaches to business—however, do take appropriate advice to make sure you are staying on the right side of the law.

Vehicle Tax

In many jurisdictions, car tax is payable. This is in essence an annual levy to keep the car on the road, and often proof of payment is shown by displaying a disk in the windshield or a sticker on the license plate. Of course, cars also get taxed in a number of other ways—for instance, sales tax when they are first sold, tax on insurance, tax on gasoline, and tax on repairs.

Insurance and Public Liability

Many employers, individuals, charities, and other organizations are required to have insurance cover various situations. A good insurance broker will be able to advise you about your liabilities. Very often, you will need to have insurance in one or more of the following areas:

■ Motor vehicle insurance. Often you will be required to have third-party insurance on any motor vehicle to insure against the injuries that you (or anyone from your organization) inflicts on someone else in a motor vehicle accident. You may also want to cover yourself for fire, theft, and damage done to your vehicle, but this is of secondary importance—the real costs will come if you injure another person.

- Public liability insurance. If the public are on property for which you are responsible (your office, a venue you have hired, and so on), then you may be responsible for any injuries sustained. Equally, you may be required to take this sort of insurance if you are taking on staff.

Although it is not a legal requirement, you may also want to take insurance against other eventualities:

- Fire and theft. As a musician you will be reliant on the tools of your trade, so you may want to insure these (and the other assets of your business) against fire and theft.

- Unexpected occurrences on tour. When you tour you will have invested a lot of money. If you can't play a gig—perhaps due to illness or other unforeseen eventuality—then you will still have to pay the expenses, but you won't have any income (because you will have to refund the tickets). For smaller gigs you can probably eat the cost, but as you start to play bigger gigs, you may want to look at insurance.

This is just a short list. I'm sure your insurance broker will be able to sell insurance for many other eventualities. Some of this may be worthwhile (for instance, life insurance), while other insurance may be useless (for instance, employment protection insurance, which has no purpose when you are self-employed), so it is probably worth the time to find a broker who specializes in the entertainment field.

Data Protection

In certain jurisdictions (in particular, the European Union), there are specific requirements around the holding of personal data (which could include names, addresses, and so on of people on your mailing list or who have purchased items from you). These requirements relate to the protection of personal data, both how you should physically protect it and how you should protect it in terms of whom you disclose it to.

You should be aware that legislative standards within the European Union for data protection are higher than they are in many other parts of the world, in particular, the United States. Therefore, if you are a European Union citizen and you ever wish to transfer personal data to the U.S. you will need to require additional security measures to be put in place by the party to whom the data is being transferred.

Criminal Records Bureau

In the world of music, often some members of the audience can be comparatively young, even (especially?) if the music embraces adult themes. Although you would not usually have a duty of care for your audience, there will clearly be occasions when some members of your organization may be able to act in a position of power in relation to your audience (for instance, they may be able to grant backstage access).

Such power can be abused. Given the potential youth of your audience, you may wish to consider whether to run a check on individuals within your organization with the specific purpose of checking for any crimes involving children.

Age, Gender, Disability, and Race Discrimination

Most jurisdictions outlaw various forms of discrimination, including discrimination in the workplace on the grounds of:

- Age
- Gender
- Disability
- Race

Often the legislation is framed in a way that the complainant does not have to prove discrimination, but rather the employer has to prove that there has not been discrimination. As soon as you start thinking about hiring people, you should consult a lawyer about any issues you should be aware of.

U.S. Copyright

In most jurisdictions there is no requirement to register copyright. There is no requirement to register a copyright in the U.S., but if you don't register, then you can't launch a claim for breach of copyright.

There used to be several forms to use in connection with registration—today there is just one, which is reproduced here. You can fill in that form by hand or you can fill it in online and submit it electronically. For further details about the requirements, you can check out the electronic Copyright Office (eCO) at copyright.gov/eco (see Figure 6.1). Copies of the forms to apply to register copyright in the U.S. and explanatory notes are included at the end of this chapter.

Figure 6.1 You can register your U.S. copyrights at the electronic Copyright Office.

Performing Rights/Mechanical Rights Organizations

Whenever a song is made or played, the song owner should get paid. There are two main rights:

- Mechanical rights. When a song is physically reproduced (for instance, a CD is made), a mechanical right is created, and the owner of the recording receives a payment (which differs by jurisdiction).

- Performance rights. When a song is played (either as part of a live performance or when a sound recording is played, whether on the television, radio, or internet), the songwriter is paid a royalty (which again varies by jurisdiction).

These royalties are collected by various (usually nonprofit) organizations around the world that collect and redistribute royalties within their jurisdiction. Clearly, you may need to join a number of organizations to get global coverage. Here is an introduction to some of the larger organizations.

When you start performing your own material and you release your own recordings, you should register with the appropriate organizations in your jurisdiction and seek advice from those organizations about registering with overseas organizations.

BMI

Broadcast Music, Incorporated (usually called the BMI; bmi.com) is a U.S. performing rights organization. It collects license fees on behalf of songwriters, composers, and music publishers, which it then distributes as royalties.

American Society of Composers, Authors and Publishers

The American Society of Composers, Authors and Publishers (usually called ASCAP; ascap.com) is a performance rights organization that collects licensing fees from users of music created by ASCAP members.

SESAC

SESAC (sesac.com; originally called the Society of European Stage Authors & Composers) is the smallest of the three performance rights organizations in the United States. However, it does claim a more personal relationship with songwriters and publishers, and unlike ASCAP and BMI, SESAC does retain some income as profit.

Harry Fox Agency

The Harry Fox Agency (harryfox.com) is the agency in the United States collecting and distributing mechanical license fees on behalf of music publishers.

MCPS-PRS Alliance

The MCPS-PRS Alliance (mcps-prs-alliance.co.uk) is an alliance between the U.K. MCPS (Mechanical Copyright Protection Society) and U.K. PRS (Performing Right Society), the two U.K. collection societies.

Society of Composers, Authors and Music Publishers of Canada

SOCAN (the Society of Composers, Authors and Music Publishers of Canada; socan.ca) is the Canadian copyright organization that administers (on behalf of its members) the right to communicate to the public and publicly perform musical works, and collects royalties accordingly.

The following pages contain the U.S. Application for Copyright Registration form and explanatory notes. You can use these to register with the U.S. Copyright Office; alternatively, you can register online at copyright.gov/eco.

UNITED STATES COPYRIGHT OFFICE
Form CO · Application for Copyright Registration

Print Form

APPLICATION FOR COPYRIGHT REGISTRATION

* Designates Required Fields

1 WORK BEING REGISTERED

1a. * Type of work being registered (*Fill in one only*)

☐ Literary work   ☐ Performing arts work

☐ Visual arts work   ☐ Motion picture/audiovisual work

☐ Sound recording   ☐ Single serial issue

ApplicationForCopyrightRegistration

1b. * Title of this work (*one title per space*)

Remove

WorkTitles

Click here to create space to add an additional title

1c. For a serial issue: Volume _____   Number _____   Issue _____   ISSN _____

1d. Previous or alternative title

1e. * Year of completion ____

Publication (*If this work has not been published, skip to Section 2*)

1f. Date of publication _____   (*mm/dd/yyyy*)   **1g.** ISBN _____

1h. Nation of publication   ☐ United States   ☐ Other   [Clear Response]   Other _____

1i. Published as a contribution in a larger work entitled

1j. If line 1i above names a serial issue   Volume _____   Number _____   Issue _____

1k. If work was preregistered   Number PRE-_____

For Office Use Only

WorkBeingRegistered

Privacy Act Notice
Sections 408-410 of title 17 of the *United States Code* authorize the Copyright Office to collect the personally identifying information requested on this form in order to process the application for copyright registration. By providing this information you are agreeing to routine uses of the information that include publication to give legal notice of your copyright claim as required by 17 U.S.C. § 705. It will appear in the Office's online catalog. If you do not provide the information requested, registration may be refused or delayed, and you may not be entitled to certain relief, remedies, and benefits under the copyright law.

| Print Form |

UNITED STATES COPYRIGHT OFFICE
Form CO · Application for Copyright Registration

2 AUTHOR INFORMATION - Entry Number

| Remove Item |

2a. Personal name   * complete either 2a or 2b

First Name   Middle   Last

2b. Organization name

2c. Doing business as

2d. Year of birth   **2e.** Year of death

2f. *   ☐ Citizenship   ☐ United States   ☐ Other   Other
         ☐ Domicile   ☐ United States   ☐ Other   Other

2g. Author's contribution: ☐ Made for hire   ☐ Anonymous
                                   ☐ Pseudonymous   (Pseudonym is:

Continuation of Author Information

2h. * This author created (Fill in only the authorship that applies to this author)

☐ Text   ☐ Compilation   ☐ Map/technical drawing   ☐ Music
☐ Poetry   ☐ Sculpture   ☐ Architectural work   ☐ Lyrics
☐ Computer program   ☐ Jewelry design   ☐ Photography   ☐ Motion picture/audiovisual
☐ Editing   ☐ 2-dimensional artwork   ☐ Script/play/screenplay   ☐ Sound recording/performance

Other:

For Office Use Only   ⑦

AuthorInformation

| Click here to create space to add an additional author |

UNITED STATES COPYRIGHT OFFICE
Form CO · Application for Copyright Registration

Print Form

3 COPYRIGHT CLAIMANT INFORMATION   - Entry Number

Remove Item

First Claimant *complete either 3a or 3b*

3a. Personal name

First Name	Middle	Last

3b. Organization name

3c. Doing business as

3d . Street address (line 1)

Street address (line 2)

City	State	ZIP / Postal code	Country

Email	Phone number

3e. If claimant is **not** an author, copyright ownership acquired by: ☐ Written agreement ☐ Will or inheritance ☐ Other   Clear

Other

For Office Use Only   ⑦

CopyrightClaimantInformation

Click here to create space to add an additional claimant

UNITED STATES COPYRIGHT OFFICE

Form CO · Application for Copyright Registration

Print Form

4 LIMITATION OF COPYRIGHT CLAIM

Skip section 4 if this work is all new.

4a. Material excluded from this claim *(Material previously registered, previously published, or not owned by this claimant)*

☐ Text   ☐ Artwork   ☐ Music   ☐ Sound recording/performance   ☐ Motion picture/audiovisual

Other: [   ]

4b. Previous registration(s)   Number [   ]   Year [   ]

                      Number [   ]   Year [   ]

4c. New material included in this claim *(This work contains new, additional, or revised material)*

☐ Text   ☐ Compilation   ☐ Map/technical drawing   ☐ Music

☐ Poetry   ☐ Sculpture   ☐ Architectural work   ☐ Lyrics

☐ Computer program ☐ Jewelry design   ☐ Photography   ☐ Motion picture/audiovisual

☐ Editing   ☐ 2-dimensional artwork ☐ Script/play/screenplay ☐ Sound recording/performance

Other: [   ]

For Office Use Only 🗗

LimitationOfCopyrightClaim

---

5 RIGHTS AND PERMISSIONS CONTACT

☐ Check if information below should be copied from the **first** copyright claimant

First Name [   ]   Middle [   ]   Last [   ]

Name of organization [   ]

Street address [   ]

Street address (line 2) [   ]

City [   ]   State [   ]   ZIP / Postal code [   ]   Country [   ]

Email [   ]   Phone Number [   ]

UNITED STATES COPYRIGHT OFFICE
Form CO · Application for Copyright Registration

Print Form

For Office Use Only   [?]

RightsAndPermissionsContact

6 CORRESPONDENCE CONTACT

☐ Copy from **first** copyright claimant   ☐ Copy from rights and permissions contact

* First Name	Middle	* Last

Name of organization

* Street address

Street address (line 2)

* City	State	ZIP / Postal code	Country

* Email	* Daytime phone number

For Office Use Only   [?]

CorrespondenceContact

UNITED STATES COPYRIGHT OFFICE
Form CO · Application for Copyright Registration

Print Form

7 MAIL CERTIFICATE TO:

☐ Copy from **first** copyright claimant   ☐ Copy from rights and permissions contact   ☐ Copy from correspondence contact

* First Name

Middle

* Last

Name of organization

* Street address

Street address (line 2)

* City

State

ZIP / Postal code

Country

For Office Use Only   ☐

MailCertificateTo

UNITED STATES COPYRIGHT OFFICE
Form CO · Application for Copyright Registration

8 CERTIFICATION

17 U.S.C. § 506(e): Any person who knowingly makes a false representation of a material fact in the application for copyright registration provided for by section 409, or in any written statement filed in connection with the application, shall be fined not more than $2,500.

I certify that I am the author, copyright claimant, or owner of exclusive rights, or the authorized agent of the author, copyright claimant, or owner of exclusive rights, of this work, and that the information given in this application is correct to the best of my knowledge.

8a. Handwritten signature

⦿ Today's date   ◯ Write date by hand

8b. Printed name   **8c.** Date signed

8d. Deposit account number   Account holder

8e. Applicant's internal tracking number (optional)

For Office Use Only

Certification

What are these barcodes for?

The Adobe® LiveCycle® Barcoded Forms bar-codes provide a facility to automate the extraction of data from paper forms and deliver it to core systems for processing. This dramatically reduces costs, **errors,** and time compared to manual data entry and solutions based on optical character recognition (OCR).

Privacy Act Notice
Sections 408-410 of title 17 of the *United States Code* authorize the Copyright Office to collect the personally identifying information requested on this form in order to process the application for copyright registration. By providing this information you are agreeing to routine uses of the information that include publication to give legal notice of your copyright claim as required by 17 U.S.C. § 705. It will appear in the Office's online catalog. If you do not provide the information requested, registration may be refused or delayed, and you may not be entitled to certain relief, remedies, and benefits under the copyright law.

UNITED STATES COPYRIGHT OFFICE
Form CO · Instructions

Use this form to register a

- *Literary work*
- *Visual arts work*
- *Performing arts work*
- *Motion picture or other audiovisual work*
- *Sound recording*
- *Single serial issue*

Before you register your work

Review the appropriate circulars on the Copyright Office website, www.copyright. gov, for detailed information about how to register particular types of works and the requirements for what copy or copies of your work to send. Also, consider using the electronic Copyright Office (eCO) for faster service and a lower filing fee.

What may be included

The following may be included in one registration on Form CO:

- ***Unpublished works:*** *works by the same author(s) and owned by the same copyright claimant(s), organized in a collection under a collection title.*

- ***Published works:*** *works published in a single unit of publication and owned by the same copyright claimant.*

What to send

1 Completed and signed application
2 $45 filing fee payable to *Register of Copyrights*
3 Deposit — the required copy or copies of your work
   - *Unpublished works:* one complete copy.
   - *Published works:* generally, two complete copies of the "best edition." There are exceptions for certain types of works. See Circular 1, *Copyright Basics*, for details.

Send all three elements in the same envelope or package to:

*Library of Congress
Copyright Office
101 Independence Avenue, SE
Washington, DC 20559-*****

Use the appropriate four-digit zip code extension to expedite the processing of your claim. In place of ****, use the following:

*Literary work: -6222
Visual arts work: -6211
Performing arts work: -6233
Motion picture/AV work: -6238
Sound recording: -6237
Serial issue: -6226*

How to use this 2D barcode form

- Complete this form online and then print it out. Do not attempt to print out a blank form. (Form CO is available only online.)

- Print out a second copy for your records. Do not save the form online.

- *Never alter the form by hand after you print it out.* The information you enter is stored in the barcodes on the form.

- If you want to make more than one registration with similar information, keep the form open after you print it; then make the necessary changes and print that version. Repeat as needed. Once you close the form, all the information entered will be lost.

- Both single- and double-sided printing is acceptable.

- *Important printer information:* To achieve best results, use a laser printer. Inkjet printer copies require enlarging if you use the shrink-to-fit-page option. Dot-matrix printer copies are not acceptable.

Line-by-line Instructions   *indicates required fields.   ** indicates required alternate fields (one of two required).

Section 1 - Work Being Registered

1A* *Type of work being registered* · Check the appropriate box. If your work contains more than one type of authorship, choose the type for the predominant authorship in the work.

1B* *Title of work* · Give only one title in this space. To enter an additional title(s), such as titles of individual works in an unpublished collection or works owned by the same claimant in a single unit of publication, click the "additional title" button. Repeat as needed, up to a maximum of 50 titles. (For a registration with more than 50 titles, file electronically or request the appropriate paper application with continuation sheets by mail. See also 1D and 1I below. Give the complete title exactly as it appears on the copy. If there is no title on the copy, give an identifying phrase to serve as the title or state "untitled." Use standard title capitalization without quotation marks; for example, The Old Man and the Sea.

1C *Serial issue* · For serials only, give the required information. **NOTE:** For copyright registration purposes, a serial is a work issued or intended to be issued in successive parts bearing numerical or chronological designations and intended to be continued indefinitely. The classification "serial" includes periodicals, newspapers, magazines, bulletins, newsletters, annuals, journals, proceedings of societies, and other similar works. Enter the ISSN (International Standard Serial Number) without dashes. The Copyright Office does not assign these numbers. For information on obtaining an ISSN, go to *www.loc.gov/issn/*.

1D *Previous or alternative title* · If the work is known by another title, give that title here.

1E* *Year of completion* · Give the year in which creation of *the work you are submitting* was completed. Do not give a year for earlier or later versions. If the work has been published, the year of completion cannot be later than the year of first publication.

1F–1H *Date of publication* · Give the complete date, in mm/dd/yyyy format, on which the work was first published. Do not give a date that is in the future. **NOTE:** Leave this line blank if the work is unpublished. "Publication" is the distribution of copies or phonorecords of a work to the public by sale or other transfer of ownership or by rental, lease, or lending. The offering to distribute copies or phonorecords to a group of persons for purposes of further distribution, public performance, or public display constitutes publication. A public performance or display of a work does not of itself constitute publication. 17 U.S.C. § 101.

1G. *ISBN* · Give the International Standard Book Number (ISBN), if one has been assigned to this work, without dashes. The Copyright Office does not assign these numbers. For information on obtaining an ISBN, contact R.R. Bowker at *www.bowker.com*.

1H *Nation of publication* · Give the nation where the work was first published. Check "United States" in any of the following circumstances: (1) if the work was first published in the United States; (2) if the work was first published simultaneously in the United States and another country; or (3) if the work was first published

in another country that is not a "treaty party," and published in the United States within 30 days of first publication. A treaty party is a country other than the United States that is a party to an international copyright agreement. Almost all countries of the world are currently treaty parties. See Circular 38a, *International Copyright Relations of the United States*, for more information. **NOTE:** Leave this line blank if the work is unpublished.

1I *Published as a contribution in a larger work entitled* · If this work has been published as part of a larger work, enter the title of that larger work in this space. Examples of a work published as part of a larger work include a song on a CD, an article in a magazine, and a poem in an anthology. If the larger work includes a volume, number, and/or issue date, add that information on the lines provided.

Section 2 - Author Information

2A** *Personal name* · Complete line 2A *or* line 2B but not both. The individual who actually created the work is the author except in the case of a "work made for hire," as explained below at 2G. Complete line 2A if the author is an individual. Give the fullest form of the name and skip line 2B.

2B** *Organization name* · Complete line 2A *or* line 2B but not both. Complete line 2B only if the work is made for hire and a corporation or organization is the author. "Work made for hire" is explained below at 2G. Give the fullest form of the corporate or organizational name.

2C *Doing business as* · You may give the name under which an author does business (doing business as; trading as; sole owner of; also known as).

2D *Year of birth* · Give the year the author was born. The year of birth is optional but is very useful as a form of author identification. Many authors have the same name. **NOTE:** If the year of birth is provided, it will be made part of the online public records produced by the Copyright Office and accessible on the Internet. This information cannot be removed later from those public records.

2E *Year of death* · This information is required if the author is deceased.

2F *Citizenship/domicile* · Check to indicate U.S. citizenship. If the author is a citizen of another country, enter the name of this nation. Alternatively, identify the nation where the author is domiciled (resides permanently).

2G *Author's contribution is* · If this line is applicable, check only one box.

- *Made for hire* · Check this box only if the work was made for hire. This means that:

  1 the work, or an author's contribution to the work, is prepared by an employee as a regular part of his or her employment, or

2   a work is specially ordered or commissioned in certain instances: for use as a contribution to a collective work, as a part
of a motion picture or other audiovisual work, as a translation,
as a supplementary work, as a compilation, as an instruc-
tional text, as a test, as answer material for a test, or as an at-
las, providing the parties agree in writing that the contribution shall be considered a work made for hire. **NOTE:** In this
case, name the employer as the author in line 2A or 2B. The
employee should not be given. See Circular 9, *Works Made
for Hire Under the 1976 Copyright Act*, for more information.

- *Anonymous* · Check this box if no natural person is named as
author on copies of the work and the work is not made for hire.
In this case, at line 2A, you should either (1) give the author's legal name or (2) state "anonymous" in the "first name" field. Do
not leave line 2A blank. If the name is given in line 2A, it will be
made part of the online public records produced by the Copyright Office and accessible on the Internet. This information
cannot be removed later from those public records.

- *Pseudonymous* · Check this box if the author is identified on
copies of the work only under a fictitious name and the work is
not made for hire. In this case, check the box and give the pseudo-
nym on the associated line. At line 2A, you should either (1) give
the author's legal name or (2) state "anonymous" in the "first
name" field. Do not leave line 2A blank. If the name is given in
line 2A, it will be made part of the online public records produced
by the Copyright Office and accessible on the Internet. This
information cannot be removed later from those public records.

2H✱ *This author created* · Check the appropriate box(es) that de-
scribe this author's contribution to this work. Give a brief statement
on the line after "other" only if it is necessary to give a more specific
description of the authorship or if none of the check boxes applies.
Examples of other authorship statements are choreography, musical
arrangement, translation, dramatization, or fictionalization. **NOTE:**
Do not give any of the following terms: idea, process, procedure,
system, method of operation, concept, principle, discovery, title, or
name. These terms refer to elements not subject to copyright. For
information on compilations, see the instructions for line 4C.

For a single serial issue, the preferred description of the authorship
is typically "collective work." Give this statement at the "other" line.
This indicates that the claim is in the collective work as a whole and
may include text, editing, compilation, and contribution(s) in which
copyright has been transferred to the claimant.

For sound recordings and musical works: Sound recordings and
musical works are separate works. To register a claim in both,
the copyright claimant(s)/owner(s) must be the same. This
requirement generally means the author(s) must be the same.
The author of a sound recording is the performer or producer,
and the authorship is "sound recording/performance." The
author of a musical work—a song, for example—is the composer
or song writer and the authorship is "music" or "music and
lyrics." See Circular 56A, *Copyright Registration of Musical
Compositions and Sound Recordings*, for more information.

Additional authors · To add another author, click the "additional
author" button. Repeat as needed.

Section 3 - Copyright Claimant Information

3A✱✱ *Personal name* · Complete line 3A *or* line 3B but not both.
Complete line 3A if the claimant is an individual. The copyright
claimant (owner) is either the author of the work or the person or
organization to whom the copyright has been transferred by an author or other authorized copyright owner. Give the fullest form of
the name and skip line 3B.

3B✱✱ *Organization name* · Complete line 3A *or* line 3B but not
both. Complete line 3B if the claimant is a corporation or organization. The copyright claimant (owner) is either the author of the
work or the person or organization to whom the copyright has
been transferred by an author or other authorized copyright owner.
Give the fullest form of the corporate or organizational name.

3C *Doing business as* · You may give the name under which a
claimant does business (doing business as; trading as; sole owner of;
also known as).

3C *Address, email, and phone* · Give this information in the lines
provided. **NOTE:** The claimant postal address will be made part
of the online public records produced by the Copyright Office and
accessible on the Internet. This information cannot be removed
later from those public records. The email address and phone
number will not appear in the public record unless also included
in section 5, Rights and Permissions Contact. Be sure to review
section 5 accordingly.

3E *Copyright ownership acquired by* · If the claimant is the author
of the work, skip this line. Transfer information is required if this
claimant is not an author but has obtained ownership of the copyright from the author or another owner. In this case, check the
appropriate box to indicate how ownership was acquired. **NOTE:**
"Written agreement" includes a transfer by assignment or by contract. "Will or inheritance" applies only if the person from whom
copyright was transferred is deceased. If necessary, check "other"
and give a brief statement indicating how copyright was transferred.

Additional claimants · To add another claimant, click the "additional claimant" button. Repeat as needed.

Section 4 - Limitation of Copyright Claim

NOTE: Skip this section unless this work contains or is based on
previously registered or previously published material, material
in the public domain, or material not owned by this claimant. The
purpose of section 4 is to exclude such material from the claim and
identify the new material upon which the present claim is based.

4A *Material excluded from this claim* · Check the appropriate box
or boxes to exclude any previously registered or previously published material, material in the public domain, or material not
owned by this claimant. "Text" may include fiction or nonfiction
text, computer program code, lyrics, poetry, or scripts. "Artwork"

may include two- or three-dimensional artwork, technical draw-ings, or photographs. "Audiovisual work" may include video clips, motion picture footage, or a series of images on a CD-ROM. (See the shaded box at the bottom of page 4 for specific examples.) Give a brief statement on the line after "other" only if it is necessary to give a more specific description of the material excluded from this claim or if none of the check boxes applies. **NOTE:** To use someone else's material in your work lawfully, you must have permission from the copyright owner of that material.

4B *Previous registration* · If the work for which you are now seek-ing registration, or an earlier version of it, has been registered, give the registration number and the year of registration. If there have been multiple registrations, you may give information regarding the last two.

> *Special situation* · If you are registering the first published edition of a work that is identical to a previously registered unpublished version (contains no new material not already reg-istered), check the "other" box in line 4A and state "First publica-tion of work registered as unpublished." In this case, skip line 4C.

4C *New material included in this claim* · Check the appropriate box or boxes to identify the new material you are claiming in this regis-tration. (See the shaded box at the bottom of this paage for specific examples.) Give a brief statement on the line after "other" only if it is necessary to give a more specific description of the new material included in this claim or if none of the check boxes applies. **NOTE:** "Compilation" is a work formed by the collection and assembling of preexisting materials or of data that are selected, coordinated, or ar-ranged in such a way that the resulting work as a whole constitutes an original work of authorship. A claim in "compilation" does not include the material that has been compiled. If that material should also be included in the claim, check the appropriate additional boxes.

Section 5 - Rights and Permissions

This is the person to contact to obtain permission to use this work. If this is the same as the first copyright claimant, simply check the box. **NOTE:** All the information given in section 5, including name, postal address, email address, and phone number, will be made part of the online public records produced by the Copyright Office and accessible on the Internet. This information cannot be removed later from those public records.

Section 6 - Correspondence Contact *

This is the person the Copyright Office should contact with any questions about this application. If this is the same as the first copy-right claimant or the rights and permissions contact, simply check the appropriate box. (Information given only in this space will not appear in the online public record.)

Section 7 - Mail Certificate To *

This is the person to whom the registration certificate should be mailed. If this is the same as the first copyright claimant, the rights and permissions contact, or the correspondence contact, simply check the appropriate box. (Information given only in this space will not appear in the online public record.)

Section 8 - Certification

8A✱ *Handwritten signature* · After you print out the completed application, be sure to sign it at this space.

8B✱ *Printed name* · Enter the name of the person who will sign the form.

8C✱ *Date signed* · Choose "today's date" or "write date by hand." In the latter case, be sure to date the application by hand when you sign it. **NOTE:** If this application gives a date of publication, do not certify using a date prior to the publication date.

8D *Deposit account* · Leave this line blank unless you have a Copy-right Office deposit account and are charging the filing fee to that account.

8E *Applicant's internal tracking number* · Enter your own internal tracking number, if any.

Section 4 — Examples

Your work	How to complete line 4a *(excluded material)*	How to complete line 4c *(new, additional, or revised material)*
New arrangement of a public domain song	Check the "text" and "music" boxes.	State "new arrangement" at the "other" line.
Revised version of a previously published book	Check the "text" box.	Check the "text" box.
English translation of a Spanish novel	Check the "text" box.	State "English translation" at the "other" line.
Movie based on a previously registered screenplay	Check the "text" box.	State "All other cinematographic material" at the "other" line.

Index